THE MAGI

FROM AN ANGEL'S

VIEW

Janis G. McReynolds, Ph.D.

*Magic must be
passed around,
Janis G. McReynolds*

It Takes 2 Publishers, Ltd.
P.O. Box 836
Gretna, NE 68028

THE MAGIC OF DEATH:
FROM AN ANGEL'S VIEW

Janis G. McReynolds, Ph.D.

Printed in the United States of America

ISBN 978-0-9818556-0-8

Published by
It Takes 2 Publishers, Ltd.
P.O. Box 836
Gretna, NE 68028

ACKNOWLEDGEMENTS

Many thanks to Rodney Lynam for his expert computer skills. Actually his abilities were heaven sent and totally unexpected---both to him and to me. The stories he could tell….

Much appreciation and thanks to Jan Marcotte for over ten years of listening to my essays, and for her many words of encouragement and praise. Earthly angels are more than friends.

I'll always remember and thank Phyllis Weichenthal for her editing and for her constant support and praise. Believing in angels and signs and heavenly messages was most helpful.

And God bless all those who passed through my life and listened to my stories over many, many years and whom I have forgotten to mention.

SPECIAL THANKS:

To all the John's in my heavenly world;
To Daddy and Mama;
And to all my many, many fleets of
Angels (both heavenly and earthly)
Who protect, love, and support me
Time after time after time

ABOUT THE AUTHOR

Janis G. McReynolds, Ph.D., was a psychology professor and business education teacher. Her dissertation (University of Nebraska-Lincoln) looked at much needed death education for medical students and that which practicing internal medicine specialists thought was necessary. She has also co-authored articles on death education for pharmaceutical journals. She has a master's degree in business education (University of Nebraska-Lincoln) and in guidance and counseling (Creighton University, Omaha).

Dr. McReynolds lives in the Midwest and is blessed with the ability to channel books for her invisible angel, Wise Eagle. She can be reached at jgmpapo@msn.com and looks forward to your comments.

AUTHOR'S NOTE

The Magic of Death was dictated to me by Wise Eagle, my resident angel. I am simply the recorder of his messages about how he saw me, my feelings, and my behavior at the time of my husband's death.

Wise Eagle had been dictating personal conversations to me for over a year. But then his dictation seemed to be in book form and concentrating on my husband's impending death and how magical it was.

Funny, because to me it seemed to be very painful, disorienting, extremely stressful, and not too much fun. Reading and teaching about others' death experiences was one thing, but living it for myself was beyond my learning curve. But luckily the process only lasted four weeks. And then my life became something that I would never have imagined.

Throughout my 30 years of teaching, I frequently would say out loud to anyone who would listen to me, "Somebody should write a book about that topic, and it should be easy to read and understand." And luckily someone in the universe heard me. So be careful of what you ask for, as you might just get it.

In 1997 my hero and number one singer, John Denver, died in a plane crash at age 53. Much too early for me, but he left a legacy of lyrics. Many, many times his songs had saved my life, as I had struggled with chronic depression for nearly 50 years.

During 1997, I had also lost my best friend who lived next door to me and one of my favorite uncles. Having been a hospice volunteer and death educator, I knew that deaths usually occur in threes; so I waited for the third one to happen.

On September 1, 1997, I noticed three mature bald eagles circling my house and garden. They came every night at 5:30 p.m. and circled until 6 p.m. If I was in the house, they swooped very close to my windows. It was almost like they needed me to notice them.

AUTHOR'S NOTE

I told no one about the eagles, as I was in a state of shock from the two deaths that I had already experienced. And since my best friend had lived next door to me, I couldn't go anywhere in my yard or my house without seeing her vacant home and remembering how much she had meant to me. But the eagles kept appearing, and I just knew that the third death was going to be spectacular.

The last night the eagles came to visit me was October 12, 1997. They came at 5:30 p.m. and left at 6 p.m. John Denver died at 5:28 p.m. (Pacific Time), and the eagles never returned.

What a powerful spiritual message! And I must add that I had lived in Nebraska my entire life and had never seen one eagle in the state, far less three who wanted to get up close and personal. Three major deaths in one year were unbearable, and I fell into a very deep depression. Many years later I learned that due to amino acid and hormonal imbalances within my body, I was unable to benefit from medication. So I suffered immensely, and so did my friends and family. Counseling helped but not a whole lot.

In January, 1998, not knowing how or where to get the help that I so desperately needed, I simply asked for what I wanted from the universe and from all of my loved ones in heaven. It went something like this, "Daddy, Mama, John (all of my most favorite men in my life had the same name), everybody in heaven, help!! If you don't send somebody to help me tomorrow, I am not staying on this planet one more day. And if I have to stay here, I need to have a dream for the rest of my life, so tell me what to do."

The next morning I got up, sat down on the toilet, looked up and saw this male angel kneeling down in front of me. All I could think of was that my sister had frequently told me to be careful of what I asked for, and this time I had gotten it. So I asked a whole bunch of what seemed to be dumb questions. Like, "How did you get here? How long are you staying?"

AUTHOR'S NOTE

He replied, "Your dad went to a LOT OF TROUBLE to get me to come be with you. And I am going to stay here with you until you die, and <u>this time</u> I'll go with you." Let's face it, I couldn't have dreamed up these answers if I stayed awake 24 hours a day for the rest of my life. And angel's answers are always profound, insightful, and far out.

And then I asked, "Who sent the eagles before John Denver's death in 1997?" His reply was even more astounding, "Your dad sent the eagles, because he knew you'd need lots of help." Talk about goose bumps up and down my spine and cold chills—I still get them when I reiterate this story. And need I tell you that my dad, John, died exactly 22 years before John Denver? But better still is the fact that my favorite Uncle John, died exactly 22 years before my dad, John.

Therefore, I knew that I was being blessed with a huge gift; but why? And from this entity's answers, I got the sense that he and I had been in each other's lives many times before.

Throughout Wise Eagle's messages that year, he talked about getting me up to speed and about my need to hurry up. I had already retired from teaching and didn't see myself doing anything too big and too spectacular. And I definitely didn't want anything that sounded like a nine-to-five job—ever, ever again.

My angel told me that I was going to be given a job of love but that first I had to agree to some specific things. I told him that I didn't want his job as it sounded like all the ones that I had already had. His reply in no uncertain terms was, "**<u>NOT!!</u>**"

Need I elaborate on his marvelous sense of humor, timing, and smart-ass remarks? And as you read this book, you'll soon see what I mean. He dictates a mean book that is full of understanding, great compassion, and a huge need for world peace.

His terms were that I could make a living from my gift of love (better known as a writing career), but that I couldn't flaunt it and try to be bigger and better than any other human being. And more importantly I had to give back the majority of my earnings to help others less fortunate than me. In other words, I was given a gift that I had to serve. Being naïve, I agreed to everything; and I am so pleased that I did.

So what about my having to hurry up and get up to speed that I heard about nearly every day of 1998 and the early part of 1999? When my husband, James Edwin, died on June 10, 1999, I knew what Wise Eagle had meant. Oh, and by the way, my dad had died on this very same day, but 22 years before.

At that moment my life began to accelerate and to go off in a totally different direction. I had never expected to be a widow at 61 years of age. Silly me, all my death lectures had talked about having to stand alone and to recreate lives. But I never saw myself in this light.

And so I quickly found that I didn't fit into any of the thousands of books that I had read on death education. No book talked about the death of a favorite entertainer, and my grieving for my husband did not seem to be too normal either.

Thus, *The Magic of Death*, became my textbook or my journal of how I lived and survived but written from an observer's point of view, Wise Eagle's. And I strongly encourage each of my readers to write a similar story or book about his painful life experiences. Someone else's grieving process is just that—someone else's. And you are not someone else.

Each of you is a very, very special angel on earth. And every story is a teaching moment for you and your loved ones. Don't let any aspect of the dying process pass by without realizing that all of it is magic and all of it is true. It's you and the magic that you spread during your time on earth. Make sure everyone knows this and notices how special it is, because the magic is you.

THE MAGIC OF DEATH:
FROM AN ANGEL'S VIEW

TABLE OF CONTENTS

CONTENTS
THE MAGIC OF DEATH: FROM AN ANGEL'S VIEW

CONTENTS
THE MAGIC OF DEATH: FROM AN ANGEL'S VIEW

PREFACE
LET ME TELL YOU ABOUT THE MAGIC OF DEATH

(**Angel's note**: Please be advised that English is no longer my first language. And, since I like to write as though I were speaking specifically to each of you, I must warn you that sometimes my grammar and spelling are different from yours. And, personally, I don't think that it matters, just as long as you hear my angel love and know that what I say is true from my vantage point here in a new and different time. And, oh, yes, I love to make up words when I can no longer remember yours. Please smile, giggle, and let your mind and imagination run wild. And may you always be free to feel the magic.)

This is a book for survivors and was written or dictated by a very loving and caring angel. And this author truly believes that what she has heard not only has helped her, but it also seems to carry a vast universal meaning. And therein is its magic.

This book is about life. It is a book about what angels can do and will do for you for free—if you will just ask, look, and listen for their wise answers. It is all about you and me together, and how I can make your day better. And it is about death, too.

It is a book about the feelings surrounding death. It is a pathway to a special place so that you can gleefully say, "Yes, since birth and life are so magical, then dying and whatever is beyond has to be the ultimate magic of this simple process called my life."

It is a book that tells you that you have just lived through a miraculous experience, your loved one's script for his earthly life. You played a role, and so did he. Now his has ended, and he has just moved to a different stage.

Your life's role is now reappearing in a new and better format. And the magic is in the fact that your life is once again just beginning; and, therefore, your new role is being massively rewritten. You see, now your life script is being played out on a stage that is new to you and being constructed specifically for you.

PREFACE

In your loved one's life, there was a role that included you. But now he's changed form, and in a sense so have you. Now he is omnipresent; something that he never was in life. Even though he was quite magical when he was alive, now in death he has gone beyond magic.

See him, touch him, feel him spiritually and know that all is well and according to plan. Guess whose plan? Maybe it is yours, too, although you cannot remember reading about it before this lifetime.

One day, another day, all will be revealed to you. And then you, too, will truly understand the meaning of you and me together and the magic that is life and death.

Sunshine on my shoulder leads me all the way to you
It's like the love of kindness of all that's right and true
To me the other wanderings
Are simply not the same
There's truth in love and laughter
There's also room for pain
What's the difference when there's none
What's the difference if we're all the same
Perhaps this ever-after
Is all that's blowing in the wind
If there's to be sun and flowers
If there's to be rain and pain
Then here's the way to ever-after
Through all the sunshine and the rain

Wise Eagle

INTRODUCTION
THE MAGIC OF DEATH

There once was a lady who loved a man so much that she gave him her heart, her mind, and her soul. Then he told her that he needed her to be his eyes, his hands, and his mouth. She said, "Sure, o. k.; I can be that." But little did she know that her life would forever be changed to one of magic.

Then she asked for a dream—you know, just something simple to hold on to. No problem; one magical gift coming up. Little did she know what she was doing, because when you truly ask a spirit for magic, you get <u>big magic</u>.

This lady had lots of gifts. She was already a magical person and didn't know it. And the magic she possessed went beyond time and space. It was a gift of love. And, in addition, she was given a job of love. And now that gift of love became one to be served.

She wanted to write a book. She wanted to tell how life should work. This life was then to be the magic for the world and for all to see. It wasn't anything beyond comprehension but was just an opening of her magic box.

Well, this magic box had more locks and braces than you can imagine. There were, in addition, ropes, tape, and iron bars all over it. Wasn't an easy task to unwrap that box.

You see, this wasn't an iron box of magic but an *ever* so soft and *terribly, terribly* fragile one. All those years of her life had been entwined with harsh, hard locks, ropes, etc. And, as a result, the opening of that box became one of rather painful unwrapping.

As one iron bar was removed, the magic began to appear and to grow and grow. Each day she saw this magic of hope and love escaping from inside that box. My gosh, she became something that she only could have hoped to be—a magical lady with a job of love to do.

Even though the unwrapping was sometimes painful, the salve of hope or the magic soothed all wounds and made her big, *really big*. As her bigness grew, so did her magic. It soon became a

INTRODUCTION
THE MAGIC OF DEATH

glow, a blush, a warmth, a radiance, and a really bright light. That was the light of the magic of hope and love.

Fortunately, this magical lady loved to write and to sit with a pen in her hand. As a result, the sitting and the writing were just a vacation for her. So every day, she took a holiday through the magic of hope and love.

No problem traveling every day and doing her job of love. After all, she could be with her lover and find the magic of the world, time, space, and beyond. She was now free, wild, and full of magic. Ain't this fun being magical? You see, she was learning the magic of me.

Little did she know how magical she was or had been or could be. It was bigger than the moon! And soon that light became something that the world needed to see and to know about.

It became a window of magic and of all aspects of life that needed to be shared. She knew that the world was ready for the magic—the magic of me—and of you and me together. And it certainly was going to take magic to make everything work.

THE MAGIC BEYOND GOODBYES

(Author's note: God and all the angels love psychological good-byes. It is one of their favorite activities, to listen to your good-bye messages to your loved one. And they all wait patiently to hear that final message. Why? So they can then swoop into your life in a newer and grander way. Why wouldn't they be excited about this, as they do these things so very, very well?)

Death and good-byes go hand in hand. And separation always means that you must say your good-byes to your loved one. Not a pleasant thought to you right now. But let me ease your mind and teach you a new truth. And the truth will set you free.

When the physical body of your loved one leaves your earthly plane and goes beyond, you <u>must</u> say good-bye to that portion of your life. Without this, your psychological pain will remain in your heart and your mind and will cause you physical and mental illness. You don't deserve this!

After you have talked out your pains and sorrows, you will begin to see something very miraculous happening. You will see a new you emerge, and the color of your days will change. And then your mind and soul will be much freer, too.

The beauty of this miracle is truly magical. Once you get beyond the good-byes, your soul and spirit will be wide open to your angels and to your God. This opening then, lets us come to help you in a new and better way, every second of every day. And, thank goodness, you will no longer block the thoughts that you once believed imaginary.

At this point, you will truly feel that we are even closer to you. Your loved one will also be given permission to come into your heart and to surround your physical being in a new way.

Thus, letting go means getting back more than you ever can believe. You give your loved one permission to go on without you, but he will return in his entirety and be better able to communicate with you in a more obvious manner.

Now you say, "How will I know that my good-byes are finished?" This is immaterial! It's the process of the saying that is most important. And, in all reality, some very special folks will require you to continue your good-byes throughout your life. But your loved one will tell you when the process is completed.

You will not have the final say. Doesn't this ease your mind to know that this deceased but very special person is still ever present in your life and calling the shots for you? Let your loved one tell you when it's time for you to go on. You must know that his power and knowledge at this point in time are much more glorious than yours.

When both of you know that you have truly gone beyond the good-byes, then you can ask for everything that you need to sustain yourself. You can ask for gifts from your deceased loved one, your other angels, and from your God, too.

The best part is that now you will really know the gifts that you need from us, and will watch, look, and listen for these miracles to happen. You've asked before, but perhaps your awareness was at a lower level. But now you are truly open to our presence in your life.

Isn't this just magic? Yes! I am saying that all you need to do is to ask for whatever special gift you need for this second, minute, hour, and day. Simply tell your angels, "I need this today. Please see that I get it. This is very important for me, and I need it to continue in my life."

I need…(statements) are magic to our ears. Boy, oh, boy! Here's another dream, a wish, a need that we can fulfill. Simple! Easy! Bound to be well received! All these words are music to our ears. Of course, if you don't feel that you're receiving your special gift today, never hesitate to repeat your request over and over again.

Will you get everything that you ask for? Sure! Sometimes it may be a little different than what you actually requested. Then, all you have to do is to be terribly aware of this and look for your gift in other places. But you will always receive your request.

And after your good-byes, the gifts will become even greater than what you've wished for. You see, angels like to overdo it, too. It's such fun for us to be excessive in our gift giving.

Gifts, miracles, magic, and good-byes—all such precious commodities that are yours for the asking. Just be sure that you are ready to receive us and your presents. We hate to be ignored and brushed aside.

Why wouldn't we hate these things? We have egos, too. Why wouldn't we love to serve you? Why and how can you ignore the magic after the good-byes? Please don't do that to yourself and to us!

THE MAGIC OF A BAD DAY

(**Author's note:** Death and bad days are nearly synonymous. Does this have to be this way? No, of course not. It is all in the asking. It is all in the seeing. And it certainly is all in the believing. Believing in everything, but particularly in God, in your special angels, and eventually in yourself will soon make all the days of your life seem like a new and undiscovered type of magic. And it will be a magic that has been spun especially for you.)

Bad days! Good days! Why have any days? And right now, I can just hear your brain frantically tap dancing, back peddling, and your whole being just squirming like mad and saying, "Where is this angel swimming to now? He never ever leaves any topic in my mind untouched or any aspect of my mind unturned." Well, here I am! Mr. Answers, that's me. And my heavenly service just happens to be free.

Said and done, on your part. Yes, oh yes, my dear earthling, I am always here beside you just waiting to pounce and dying to see the look on your pretty face when I throw you another fish to chew on—or better still, have you swim with that fish.

You see, fish are the only answers to this special brand of magic—the magic of a bad day. Yes, I hear and see your mind thinking, "*Fish?* He's incorrigible and definitely not making any sense this time." Oh, how I love my doubting human being that I serve here on earth, you.

And this is my most beautiful point. I never have to make sense, because I am totally committed to making <u>no sense</u> of your earthly life, which is so hard and so misunderstood. And, yes, I remember my time on earth very, very well.

4

God just as well made you all fish, cause a bad day makes as much sense as a world made up of totally fish. *And what this angel would give for such a place!* Fish and endless streams and tons of bait and worlds of time to enjoy all of them! Now this is my kind of magic, fishing.

See, I already have you giggling about where my fish story and I are going and how it truly is magical to have a bad day. This is progress, God! This is more like how you would have your earthly lady react, giggling, instead of masses of tears and debilitating depression. A bad day on earth truly does need this fishy type of magic to succeed.

Fish and magic are both tenderly and lovingly created by God and for all the world to enjoy, too. How do I know this? Because of all the things that happened to me while I was on earth and since my timely (or untimely for you) exit to this higher plane.

Life on earth is made up of more water and fish than people and land. And then, too, there are all the psychological problems that occur in your process called life. Therefore, it is important that you realize that fish live in the vastest regions of planet earth, God's heavenly waters.

Fish see all, know all, and definitely hear all, as they can hear for many, many miles, thanks to God's creation called water. Hmmm—earth and water and fish—all of these are among my most famous and dearly-loved topics. But, all of this is for another time, as now I must get back to my fish story.

Through their keen sense of hearing, fish are able to know and to hear all sides of all conversations. And, thus, they are some of the most knowledgeable beings on the planet. But who do you know that has last talked to a fish and gotten a straight human type answer? Not many. Too bad! So much pertinent information is being wasted. No wonder men and women have so much trouble just living on planet earth.

Well, back to bad days and being a fish. How many fish have you talked to lately who have had a bad day? None! And that's my point, fish do not have bad days. Why? Because a day in the life of a fish is spent in his most favorite environment, God's steam or river or ocean.

You see, having only one environment to be concerned with is much easier. And thus the moral of my story is to tell you that in your next lifetime consider being a fish in the really big pond on Mother Earth.

Why would you want to do this? If you want the wisdom of the world (like the fish possesses), then you must live in the widest and most hostile and yet the most serene place, the watery masses on your planet.

When you do this, you are then bathed in the most beautiful water—and all the time, too. Never is your thinking hindered. Never are you in such despair that you can't function. Never are you anything but living and being beautiful in the bathtub of the world.

And then if you're really lucky, you'll have some handsome hunk or gorgeous dame come along and snag you and raise you to the surface of the water. Then you can converse with your captor and tell him about your life, your living, and what is true about your universe. And after you smile real nice, then that person will set you free so that you can then tell your tales of man's life to those who also live in the deep waters of your world.

And probably the best part of the fish's watery world is that all angelic transmissions are sent via the currents, rapids, and waves. Just think about this! The fish live and operate in the most knowledgeable place on your planet. They are always bathed in love and in the latest information of the entire universe. Bet you didn't know this.

So, the next time that you have a bad day, I challenge you to go find a fish to talk to. He will lovingly listen to your woes, watch your tears drop into and thus expand his beautiful world, and then pass on your needs to all us angels. And to all the other fish in the world, too.

Isn't this just the perfect answer to a really bad day? *Go call up a fish to talk to!* And then we can all talk extensively about your magic and how any fish can tell you the ultimate truth about the absolute and total magic out here in the universe. And this definitely means the hidden magic that is within a bad day on planet earth.

How do I know? Because I have been a fish and remember who talked to me, who was kind enough to not eat me, and who so much loved me and my environment and worked to protect me. And I'm the magical fish (now in angel form) who will love you more than anybody can.

Remember, too, that I never have a bad day. All of my days are just God's days and all are as they are meant to be. So, go look up your favorite fish and ask him to make your day better! I dream about you doing this. Won't you make my angel dreams come true? After all, aren't we all just fish out of water?

THE MAGIC OF A DISEASE

(**Author's note:** Diseases are many. Diseases are varied. But all of them produce the same effects within a survivor's life. They bring more sadness and a lot of stress, plus new and varied answers. And it is at this point that the survivor must look for his own special magic within the disease.)

All of God's children have concerns. All of God's children wonder. All of God's children worry from time to time. All of God's children have typical feelings when it comes to feeling ill. And all of God's children are pretty special, too.

So you have been physically ill, and you do not think that you are recovering too quickly. That is just the d-i-s part of the word that you know as dis-ease. And then, of course, your concern is magnified; and it just may be way out of proportion, too.

The death of a loved one always does this to the survivor. You might be thinking, "Boy, if he got sick that quickly and died, then maybe I will experience the same thing. Or, God forbid that I may even experience something much worse."

Hey, it ain't unusual to tend to overreact in situations like this. It ain't abnormal to feel this way. And ain't it nice to know that you're just normal, if there is such a thing?

But wait just a minute now. First of all, you may be feeling terrible. If you live alone, you will really wonder if you can manage on top of all your other duties. And worse still, you will somehow get around to wondering if you could become too ill to even call for help.

Now calling for help is where we work best. There should never be a doubt in your mind, as us angels are much better and *way more effective* than your 911 emergency service. And, remember that you can always depend upon us to call for help. Whew! This thought alone has got to be a relief for your very troubled mind.

Now on to just you. You have been through a hellish experience with your loved one's death, and you are mentally frazzled. And now you physically feel like shit. Why am I not surprised?

Just look back for a few moments. You have lived and grown from your loved one's death which was terribly stressful. It may have happened very quickly. It may have been a sudden accident. And now you are required to deal with all of those happenings.

Somewhere within your body, every incident, every pain, every half-second of joy have been registered. You consciously cannot remember everything that was said or done, but your cells can. Good, bad and otherwise—yes, it is all there and waiting for you to cope with it. And, no, it will not go away on its own.

And sometimes in situations like this, your body just shuts down and tells you, "No more trauma!" And that is all that an illness is. It's just your own special valve to keep you from overloading and burning yourself out. Cute device God made, huh?

When you are physically ill, you doubt. And when doubt creeps in and takes over your world, then that world gets painted a different color. Oh, it's probably a color that you can identify; but just maybe it's a non-descriptive, non-recognizable one— something like the color of nothingness that is associated with fear and pain.

Doctors can identify your physical illness and prescribe good medications for you. What they don't handle too well is the color of your world. And right now it's your thoughts and feelings that need special attention, too. Without this, your world can very quickly become one of pain, fear, abject fatigue, and over-whelmingness [sic].

The magic of all of this is our presence. We see, know, and can describe things to you that none other can. We can ease that dis-ease. And we can cure that special part of you that only you and us know about.

We can be your knights in shining armor. We can be your friends. We can be that lifeline back to the magic that you can understand when you are physically feeling better. We can be that vehicle back to what you call normalcy.

Just our hovering about you, just our loving presence, just our cute little quips silently whispered in your ear—all of these can make a world of difference. And our special brand of magic of just being with you all the time can make your world much different, too.

We are the magic you long for. And, yes, all of God's children have our free services. All of God's children were born having us about. All of God's children have the same benefits. And, yes, all of God's children suffer and do need our magical touches.

All of God's children deserve the best. All of God's children are just pure magic! And all of our magic is free, and we can color you back to good health. Therefore, within the magic of your disease, we live, reign, and rule.

Want to argue with me? Want to bet? Want to know the difference? All of this is our free service within your magical disease. And I can certainly bet you (and win, too) when I ask, "Ever thought about how much magic there is within your own disease? Ever wonder how large the price was for you to succumb to this illness? Want to put a dollar figure on it?"

Well, let me tell you that your earthly money cannot even begin to be used to calculate this price. Get the picture? Got an idea of what angel dollars are? Want another lesson?

Well, go ahead and ask, and we will make sure that you receive your costly answer. And it is all for free and given out of pure love and caring. Now, you surely must know that we are your year-round Christmas angels who have come to make you well. So, just lay back and let us shine—just for you and for all time.

THE MAGIC OF A LULLABY

(**Author's note:** Angels are sending lullabies to you constantly. You say they're on the wrong frequency? Whose frequency are you on? If you want to hear them, simply quietly sit and listen to the silence, to the wind, to the trees, to the world. Soon you'll hear something much different, something much like a song written just for you.)

What's more celestial than an angel singing you a lullaby? What are we better equipped to do? How glorious that you finally want to listen to a lullaby and to us.

Can you even begin to realize what this communication is like? Here are all these heavenly messages being sent to you constantly, and all the time you're generally very unaware of them.

You on earth think that what you have in your modern world is fantastic. Let me tell you that the lullabies that we are singing for you are of a much higher quality, are faster, even greater, and much vaster than anything that you can comprehend. And it's all done for free, without wires, without machines, and without conscious effort. Now try and tell me who's ahead of whom? And all of this has been going on since time immemorial.

Show me a lady who doesn't like a lullaby, and I'll personally appear before her and convince her myself. Just try and find me one! I can fulfill that mission, too.

Lullaby! What a word! Doesn't it just conjure up celestial notes and glorious melodious sounds and such fantastic musical instruments? It certainly does for me and always has.

When I come to sing you a lullaby, it may be in the form of a beautiful song that is heavenly to your ears. It may be sounds of love. It may be able to paint you a lovely picture in your mind. It may be just a picture waiting to evolve before your very eyes. It certainly may be a moment of love.

On the other hand, our lullabies are sometimes sent in different formats. Because you cannot always hear the music that we play just for you, we must then resort to other forms of communication.

In your world, this may be in the form of signs and symbols. It may be unusual happenings in your life. It may be things that challenge you to interpret them. It may be just our efforts to use all our technology to get through to you.

Everyone has the God-given talent to communicate with angels and spirits and God. Some find this frightening. Others find it extremely uplifting and comforting and supportive. I hope the latter is true for you. Then this will make my task much easier.

For those of you who like the written word, it can be in the form of books and other literary things. Some prefer to see a hard copy of our words. This is quite o.k., too. Always remember to read yourself into every word of that book or essay.

We also like very much to whisper in people's ears. That's always a great way for us to hone up our word skills and to stay in contact with your vocabulary and your thoughts, feelings, and ideas. Have you really thought about whispering for a long time?

Little folks always whisper, but somehow big people have gotten away from this. Whispers are delicious! Try them and become a child once again. Just get up close to a warm, caring human and softly and gently whisper in the other's ear. Bet you've forgotten how sensuous and delicious that really is!

There are also other ways that we send a lullaby. It could be in the form of a loving friend's phone call, letter, or email. All of these are messages from your angels and should be looked upon in this manner. Each time the phone rings, just imagine that it's one of us calling to tell you that we love you, care about you, and are thinking about all the best for you.

Each personal letter in your mailbox is from an angel. Each email that you receive is someone telling you, "You're special. I took time out of my busy day to send you thoughts of love. I care!"

Not all messages contain the exact words, "I love you," but in essence that is exactly what each one is symbolically saying.

The lullabies from above are ever present in every second of your life. To miss even one of them is a waste. But if you do, not to worry, as we are relentless in completing our communications from God and us to you.

We just keep hitting the repeat dial button and keep on sending. To us, not received is just another opportunity to keep redialing. We do this so easily and without any effort. And we're never going to hang up without leaving a message.

Please awaken and listen to our messages. Please let us come and comfort you at this time of turmoil in your life. Please say that you care enough about yourself and us and God to not hang up.

THE MAGIC OF A SUDDEN DEATH

(**Author's note:** When human beings think about any type of death, they usually think first about themselves and how it affects their lives and their emotions. But thinking about your loved one who has suffered a sudden and/or violent death and who is now an angel may show you some better ways of being. Remember, now his eyes are much different from yours and much more accurate in what they see.)

It's amazing that sudden death is such an abhorrent thing. Actually, it's a quick and easy way to leave this earth and to fly heavenward to God. What's wrong with this picture? Obviously, it's a picture that can only be seen by the deceased and not by the survivors. That's where the abhorrence comes into play.

Now as I look at this process with my angel eyes, the picture is perfect. The quickness of it was such a gift, such a blessing. One second all is normal as you see it on earth and then *wham*--the world suddenly becomes brighter and more picturesque. And it's certainly a glorious way to say good-bye to one lifetime and to then go be in another space.

Yes, that's my view of the process today. But in my past I, too, never looked upon it in this way. Sudden death always seemed to be a huge shock that required so much grieving and so much picking up of the pieces. And let's face it, when I was a human being, all of this was a burden for me, too.

The sudden-death process involves so many changes that happen all at once. No wonder folks feel crazy. And then these changes can hardly be seen as the gifts that they really are.

Why? Because the changes are too numerous. They are too painful. They are too permanent. And they are too detrimental to one's psyche and to one's confidence. And, in addition, they are just too difficult to understand.

But maybe understanding isn't important. Maybe the experience is all that's needed. Maybe God has just given you way too many gifts. Maybe life should be this way more frequently. Maybe you would then be better able to cope. But, on the other hand, maybe coping isn't important. And maybe believing is the key.

True and intense believing would give you the foundation to build upon. Imagine an extremely stable foundation based upon God, the spirit world, and all of your guardian angels. Now think on this a bit.

Here is this domain where all is well. Here are these loving, caring angel folks who are going to welcome you with open arms and *always* be there for you—in every way, in every situation, and in every dream that you can imagine. Isn't this really something to anticipate and to long for? Isn't this what all humans on earth want?

So, then it seems that when a loved one is plucked from your midst that you forget all about these facets of the afterlife and then begin your horrendous process of lamenting and bemoaning your loved one's fate and yours, too. Now, just what are you *really* believing in? Nothing has occurred that should ever destroy this wonderful heavenly foundation that God has built and made into something that is far more stable than Mother Earth.

Maybe the abhorrence is about your life on earth. Maybe life is the problem. Maybe believing is the problem. Maybe life should be about believing, accepting, and building upon God's foundation and accepting your life here and the one that he has planned for you in your afterlife.

Maybe your abhorrence of sudden-death situations is really a gift that should now be served and closely examined. And maybe abhorrence is God's next gift for you to own and to love. And maybe within this feeling, your angels can reveal to you the magic of the gift of your loved one's sudden death.

THE MAGIC OF A WARNING

(**Author's note:** Warnings and messages from heaven are simply love letters that the angels are sending to you. Wise Eagle has described these as feathers thrown into the wind. And, ironically, they are always sent and delivered precisely on time. A feather, a wind, and a love message—what better way to spend your time?)

Someone senses that something is about to happen. Someone hears a voice from out of the heavens that foretells the future. Someone cares enough to listen to us angels and to communicate our message to loved ones on earth. That's the magic of a beautiful warning.

Within each of you is a time clock—a timetable, a roadmap for life, a sense of knowing that the end is coming one day. Some of you can read, hear, sense, and tune in more carefully than others. But each of you has this marvelous and useful ability, if you would hone in on this skill and use it for yourself and not against yourself.

What kind of a person hears such warnings? Well, it doesn't take anyone really special. All it takes is one of God's children who cares enough about himself to tune into the universe.

A warning may come in a dream. It may come in a flash from something said on a television show. It may be something that is read in a book. Any of these things can trigger and cue into God and the angels and what they're saying. Any way that it happens, it is just such a beautiful gift for the person and for the loved ones.

The warning tells you that life is fleeting. It tells you that all is well in the world and that everything happens for a specific reason. It tells you that God's plan for you is right on schedule and that it is truly monitored from afar.

The warning tells you that God loves all of his children equally. Anyone can be the bearer of such a gift. And anyone that receives this message from a loved one can be considered truly and wonderfully blessed.

The warning also tells you that all gifts are huge. All gifts come in a variety of wrappings with appropriately attached bows. And that all gifts happen and are delivered right on schedule.

On the other hand, such a warning can be mistakenly misinterpreted. It is not a threat! It is not a bad thing! It is never and will never be punishment. It is not something blithely or whimsically sent to frighten you and to shape you up. Just who would do that to you? Not anyone that I know here in heaven.

Your reaction to such warnings depends upon on how you look at yourself, your world, and God's world. Just who is the most important person and/or entity in your earthly world?

From my vantage point, we are all equal. We are all vitally important to each other. You see, this is a universal system of you and me together. If one fails, then all fail.

And so your loved one has told you that his time is running short—that he now knows how, when, and where his death is going to occur. Do not take this lightly. Do not laugh it off. Do not panic. Do not disregard and pooh, pooh this heavenly message. To do so would be a travesty against your loved one. Do not say, "That is not true, and it will not happen."

Now is the time to get your home in order. And by the words, your home, I mean way more than your earthly interpretation. For clarity, there is your psychological home, your physical home, your parenting home, your career home, and your spiritual home. In addition, there is also and most importantly your heavenly home. Cover all these bases, and the road ahead will be all that you hope it will be.

Just the knowing that an event is going to happen is such a heavenly blessing. It is a gift that is insurmountable. It is a test of all your earthly skills. And it is also a test of our heavenly skills.

Don't you think that all of us are capable of being everything for each other? Well, let me tell you that the practiced team of angels that surrounds you is at your beckon call. Call us! We will come instantaneously.

We have skills unlimited. We are ever present. We love beyond belief. Our holding and hugging power will surpass anything you have on earth. We are just the cat's meow! And best of all, we're always free, available, and will over love you through this marvelous journey that you are embarking on.

The magic within the warning is you. You are God's magic on earth. You are all the magic that you will ever need. If you don't believe me, just ask me. I'm more than happy to come and to whisper in your ear. And actually, whispering is my best and most beloved job here in heaven.

THE MAGIC OF AN UNKNOWN SADNESS

(**Author's note:** Every death brings with it its own special type of sadness. And sometimes this sadness simply occurs when you go around a corner in your house or when you turn over in bed. It is not something that you do on purpose, but it is just a gentle bolt of heavenly lightning that strikes you and makes you pause and remember. Let's just say it is caused by angelic feathers that are tickling your tear ducts. And during these times, always talk to your angels and ask for clarification and for hidden meanings.)

Sadness and tears don't have to come from anywhere in particular. They can simply be in the air that surrounds you. You don't have to have a certain memory of your loved one.

You don't have to have anything happen to you to make you feel sad. Sadness is just magical and surrounds you like a warm and loving gentle cloak. Put on this magical garment and ride away on it.

Sadness is so magical, because it appears out of nowhere and goes nowhere. It's just a lovely floaty place to be in time. It doesn't mean that there's something wrong with you. It doesn't mean that you're going insane. It doesn't mean that you're not through grieving (trust me, you never will be). It doesn't mean that you're missing your loved one. It just means that you are you.

You can be sad just because you're alone and trying to cope, no matter how good or bad you judge your skills. And I highly suggest that you *never* try to judge these skills. That's a ticket on a train going over the edge of a cliff, for sure!

Do not buy a ticket on that ill-fated train, do not climb aboard, do not sit down in that railcar and take off into that crevasse of passing judgment on yourself. By the same token, don't let anyone else pass judgment on you either.

Just running across something that belonged to your loved one may trigger an unusual response of sadness. It might be something as simple as a piece of paper with his handwriting on it. That penmanship was one of a kind and will never come again.

Why shouldn't the sight of that bring back a flood of good and bad memories? That was a signature etched in time and more than likely in gold. It will never come again and hold the same meaning for you and for him and for your life together. All of this is just magic, as it should be.

Anything that belonged to your loved one will evoke a memory. Anything that causes you to pause and to remember may make you feel sad. Anything that the two of you shared will certainly be worth pausing for and remembering and shedding a few tears—even if those tears do not seem to be exactly connected with an event. And, as a result, you must remember that everything about sadness is just magical.

To you, magic only seems to be a glorious, breathtaking event. And that is true. And when you're feeling sad, I imagine that you're having some difficulty breathing. Sounds like magic happening to me. The glorious part then comes later when you realize that your sadness didn't happen by chance.

Every drop of sadness that you feel is there for a purpose. It is a happening that shows you the way home—home to be with God and me and all your other angels. Sadness is simply a sign that you are still alive and feeling and breathing and caring about yourself and your world.

Every tear that glides down your face tells us just what a special individual you are and how much you mean to us and to yourself. Without those tears, you would not be the human being that you were meant to be. And if you aren't the person that you were meant to be, where does this leave me? Out drying on the clothesline? If that happened, God wouldn't be happy with either of us.

You see, sadness just says that you are such a special person; and one with extraordinary skills and talents and with ones that will make the world a better place. Just look upon each of your tears as a gift from us to you. And, in return, you are giving us a gift of all the magic that is within you. Sadness and tears are just signs of hidden magic within a special person called *you*.

Let the tears flow. Let the sadness be seen. Let the world know that you are one of God's magical beings that was sent to earth for great and specific purposes.

Without this outward sign, wouldn't your friends and loved ones miss a valuable lesson for their lives? Wouldn't they be lesser individuals without your sharing of your unknown sadness and tears? Wouldn't they be missing you?

The magic of the sadness is just you and all your beauty, your talents, and your blessed gifts. Give those gifts to all—far and wide—and let's join hands in the sadness and the magic and make the world a better place. Amen!

THE MAGIC OF BEING ALONE

(**Author's note:** Being the first one to die definitely has its advantages. And being the one who is left alone does have its problems. If you are living alone for the first time in your life, you will need to draw upon some special attributes, all of which you possess; but sometimes you just can't imagine where they are.)

Being alone is magical, in and of itself. At no time are you ever more in touch with me and God than when you are physically alone. And this is the magic of just being alive and now alone.

So, it doesn't sound peaceful or pleasant to you right now. So, it isn't a comfortable place to be. So, it's not like you are anywhere at all. So, it's not a feeling of being in love. So, it's not a place of salvation.

I'd like to tell you that it's going to be better in due time. I'd like to tell you that all will be well. I'd like to tell you to relish the moment. I'd like to see you love the feeling. I'd like to see you in love with yourself. Maybe I can help.

Being alone is <u>really</u> what each human being does the very best. Just think of how your work is something that you must do in order to fulfill your job requirements. Don't you generally do this by yourself, even though you may be in the proximity of other humans?

Well, in thinking of your earthly job, can't you realize that to do this you are basically alone and still functioning all the time? Aren't you best at fulfilling your earthly tasks when you are alone, particularly psychologically, if not physically, too?

Being alone simply means being totally receptive to God's messages and to ours. Now try to tell me that you are alone when we are communicating with you. If you try to do so, I'll certainly tell you differently.

Alone after a death is sort of like emerging from a lovely cocoon where you have been resting and growing. And when you emerge, of course, you're new and bright and shiny and so vulnerable. You've lived through your loved one's death and come out the other side, so to speak.

But the other side of the mountain of death is certainly not the side that you previously lived on. The foliage has changed. The weather is brand new. The flowers also look and smell anew. And, of course, the wildlife is certainly more awesome.

So, now you're alone on a new mountainside, and you can either climb higher or slide down into a quagmire of psychological despair. Are both of these places exciting? Sure are, as both places offer you limitless opportunities, most of which you've never had before.

So, what you end up with are too many choices. And choices are simply too many feathers in the wind. And, of course, guess who gets to catch you at the bottom of that slippery slide of choices so that you don't drown in that psychological quagmire? *Me!*

The most obvious solution is to grab only one feather at a time and to read its loving message. You see, a feather in the wind is being sent to you nearly every second of your life. And just because one feather is not to your liking doesn't mean that your new nest will never be feathered again with things and people that will sustain you.

A feather is just a feather! A strong wind beneath that feather only blows your mind and makes you feel ungrounded. But remember that at no time is the wind ever too much or too little for the feathers in your life. And the wind and the feathers will bring you home.

Enjoy, love, and cherish your next precious feather. And look carefully for where you must build your next nest. The wind and the feathers are your friends and the magic of your world. And also remember that each feather arrives totally alone and is also magical.

THE MAGIC OF BEING
ANGER-LESS

(**Author's note:** At the time of a death, never allow anyone to tell you how you should feel. Every emotion that you have is coming from a very special place that is deep inside of you. And with each emotion also comes your angel's message of love. And that message will never follow another person's stages of grief. So, now you must write your own book on living through the death of a loved one. Please allow yourself to do this and to be unique, different, and magical.)

When I talk about being anger-less, I'm talking about being absolutely and totally free of any anger about your loved one's death. In other words, if you feel this way then you can freely say, "I am not angry that he died."

Sounds like an ominous task? Why should it be? Do you deserve to be angry about your loss? Do you need to waste your time on this emotion? Why not think in terms of your life and your dreams? All that has happened is that your loved one has walked off stage, and your dream for your life has simply changed.

On earth you have not been taught to think in these terms. Instead you have been told that you should be angry. I'm here to tell you that that is hogwash, a waste of time, and certainly not written into the script for your life. There is no need to learn to be angry or to expect it or to even make it happen.

Humans tend to see life as filled with stages of loss and never-ending grief. Where and how did you come up with those things? Oh, yes, I forgot. You need to put some semblance of order into your life. You need to categorize things. You need to be able to fit your emotions into someone else's pattern. Well, I'm here to tell you that the only pattern that you're following is the one that you have created, along with our help, before this lifetime.

What you're forgetting is the magic of the whole event called death. It's an experience that you will be astounded by. It's the magic of having everything become very clear to you—all your questions, all your longings, and all your magical angelic friends. Tell me what in here should cause you to be angry? Nothing!

"Death is a celebration." It's the returning of a soul to heaven. It's not the ending of your life. It's simply the beginning of a new dream for yourself. Your loved one certainly isn't angry that he has left his earthly home. Why should you be angry?

Do you deserve to beat yourself up with this useless emotion? Do you deserve to waste your time? Is this an emotion that serves you well? If it is, then we need to do some rearranging in your mind.

As an angel, I see your anger as a funny game. It's one of moving a wooden piece or object around on a silly board, something like a Monopoly board. So you stop on, or God forbid, you buy a piece of property on Angry Street. Then you tell yourself, "Hmmmm, I landed on here for a reason; and, therefore, I should buy into this land (or emotion)." I don't think so!

So let's say that you bought into this property on Angry Street. Owning such a site also means that you have to maintain it. Of course, this includes paying taxes on it, shoveling the snow, and providing all the amenities that go along with being angry. Who in the hell wants to buy into such a game-board idea? But isn't that what you do as a human on earth?

I suggest you get out your bottle of White Out or your eraser or a razor blade and wipe out that specific square on that game board. Then no one can ever land on it in the future. Gone, out of sight, no more Angry Street for you to buy into, live on, or rest upon. And, believe you me, living on Angry Street ain't even a place that you want to come close to.

If there is no such place, then no one will ever go there again, as being angry isn't a place to be. What a silly counseling idea that was! Be there, experience it, and work through it. *Why?* It doesn't even deserve to be addressed. Have every other emotion that you want surrounding your loved one's death, but please bypass anger and go on to the emotions that are really *worth* experiencing.

To me, it seems that God never wanted you to experience anger when your loved one returned to heaven and when his script or life on earth had been completed. God didn't take your loved one home. God didn't do you a disfavor or do something to make your life more difficult. God is not responsible for your loss. And what's more, death *is not* a loss.

All that has happened is that a part of your script has ended. Your loved one's life was at the end of its dream or plan. And now before you lays a whole new script that you are free to write. And it does not include some silly game called Buying Into Angry Street and living there and wasting time.

The magic of death lies within being free. You are now free of a need to be angry. You are now free of your need to be less than all you can be. Having less or no anger just gives you a license to free up yourself to welcome the gifts that your angels can bring you.

In this case, the magic truly does lie in having less—less anger that is. And having less really means having much more—much more time to ask for angel help and to let us come and be with you.

Without anger, you will hear us better. Without anger, you can ask us specifically for what you need. Without anger, we can bring you all the gifts that you so rightfully deserve.

Without anger, we can all sing together—and, by the way, sing the same song at the same time. If you're off key, not to worry. The music that we all produce seems to work—no matter in what key and even if you can't sing in any key. We will help to make more out of less. Just ask us and see what happens when you decide to have no emotion called anger.

THE MAGIC OF BEING BLOWN AWAY

(**Author's note:** One of the emotions surrounding a death situation is feeling that you have been blown away by some torrential wind that refuses to stop. And all of this is just how you are meant to feel.)

Being blown away can be a really good and exciting thing. It's like taking off from Mother Earth and soaring with the eagles. It's like laughing in the wind and giggling with the moon and stars. It's like being everywhere at once and being responsible to and for no one else. It's like being in a euphoric state where you are timeless, weightless, and free.

What have I just described? I've told you about death and the dying process. Now isn't that really and truly something that you should long for? So, what's the problem with death?

Few people view it as a gift from God and a place to long for. Most folks see it as something that destroys them and their lives. Both God and I wonder how on earth you ever got this idea.

And most folks see death as a loss. But who came up with that thought? I certainly need to have a big talk with that person.

Loss is not a word. Grief is not a word. At least they're not in God's dictionary for the universe. Therefore, man must have come up with these ideas to explain something that isn't perfect in earthly terms and for humans' needs.

Believing in God and his universe means that you also believe in his plans for eternity. And his plan only includes positive gifts and not detrimental, painful occasions.

And since life is to be lived according to God's logic—not according to man's—this means that every death is meant to be and never happens by chance. Therefore, death is simply a time for one's script to be fulfilled. And, in God's eyes, this is meant to be a time for rejoicing.

So how does feeling blown away fit into this scheme? Well, every death results in the survivors feeling that they are blown away with all the details, the decisions, and the changes. But blown away where?

Are they blown into the sea? Are they soaring with the mountain winds? Are they basking on the sunny beaches of the tropics? Probably not! In death situations, being blown away more than likely refers to feeling crazy, downtrodden, devastated, grief riddled, and in shock.

Where did those words come from? They came from man's need to put into human words the emotional aspects of the dying process. Do these words serve the purpose in today's death situations? Not in my book!

They're archaic. They're confining. And they're limiting humans from believing freely and totally in God's universe and in the spirit world. And without these firm beliefs, then death becomes an obstacle that needs to be conquered.

Instead I want you to view death as a gift of magic—a time for celebration and renewal; and a time for comfort in the fact that all's well with you, your loved one, and God. And you need to realize that your loved one's death just means that he has been blown away—blown away home.

And now you, the survivor, needs to know that your feelings of being blown away are just the right words to describe your situation. You, too, need to know that being blown away for you means being blown back into the reality and the beauty of heaven and God and the spirits. Such feelings are given to you by God so that you can be blown back into his arms and to know that you are safe there and loved.

Therefore, the magic of being blown away is the magic of God working for you and with you. And firmly believing in him and in the spirit world will again put you into direct contact with your loved one.

So, sit down and start talking with that person and know that you've all been blown back into each other's lives in a new and different dimension, one of pure communication and love. And more than likely, you've never experienced this with your loved one. Now enjoy being blown away home so that you, too, can feel the magic of where he now resides.

THE MAGIC OF BEING LOVED AND CHERISHED AGAIN

(**Author's note:** Some folks believe that there is just one person that they can be in love with. Other folks spend a great deal of time looking for the next love relationship, even though they are perfectly happy with their present mate. All I know is that daily my angel opens every door for me—every door labeled with, "This may be the next love in your life.")

What a gift to just know that there's one human being that will love, cherish, and adore you throughout your life. What a gift to just know that all's well and all right between you and one other person.

Have you had this? Would you know it and remember it? What are the chances that you will have such a being in your life again? Will you know it when this happens?

Because you remember this feeling of adoration from a past life, you have it within your cells to recall, to remember, and to cherish this emotion. It's all there; thus, the longing will always remain within you. And that longing always seems to have a special spot within your heart.

This longing for pure love is never dampened. It is never far from your mind. It is never gone from your heart and your dreams. It will always remain within you as the magic of being loved.

What does this longing do for you? Of course, it gives you a perfect dream. It gives you a gleam in your eyes. It gives you a breathless feeling of anticipation and of potential fulfillment. It gives you a flutter deep inside. And thus it basically gives you a very special part of you.

What is this magic? It's a love beyond your earthly domain. And whether or not it will come again is always one of life's mysteries. But just knowing it's a possibility will give many of your days a special color—one of radiance, luster, and great unbelievable star quality. Of course, this is your own color of love.

This magic surrounding the color of your love and your dreams is one that is known only to you. And, as a result, the color is mixed and will be blended to ease your pain and to brighten up your days.

Just knowing that the possibility always exists for you to be loved and cherished again will give your days a new type of light. And who knows, today may be that day. Today just may be the day for that experience of love to become a new reality to have and to hold. If not, don't despair, as God makes this possibility happen every second of your life.

A gift you say? A huge gift, I say. It's the magic of the gift of a possibility of love. So expect that today will be your day and that all the love will come your way. And tonight you can crawl in bed knowing that once again you are being loved and cherished.

THE MAGIC OF BELIEVING

(**Author's note:** A firm foundation is all that is needed to get you through any death situation. And believing in a very specific angel and listening to his wisdom and never doubting his love, caring, and guidance have been very important to me. I no longer have a need to be right and to know all the answers. And one of his famous sayings is, "Simple is as simple is.")

Whether or not you believe in heaven or God or angels or some other inanimate object, I guarantee you that the death of a loved one will only be tolerable if you believe in something. And that something doesn't have to be whatever someone else believes in. But you'd better believe in something, someone, or yourself.

Why do I make this so emphatic? Well, just try to live through a loved one's death and all the surrounding heartaches and pains without being a believer. It ain't a pretty picture, and it certainly is a terribly painful process for most folks.

Just strongly believing alleviates so many sad times. And I'm not even talking about the frustrating, fearful times involving other changes, losses, and utter desperations. You need the magic of believing to see you through.

This believing process is again terribly unique and one-of-a-kind and not like any other person's. It's something given to you at the moment that your spirit enters your earthly body. Of course, it's one that's been tested nearly every day of your life and all for a specific reason.

Believing is just you. Folks can try to influence and to guide you. Good luck is what I say to those folks, as believing is such an elusive, uncapturable [sic] thing.

Where does it live? Why of course, within your heart. It's that special place that's either your own prison or your very own palace. Sometimes you color it to suit your mood, your day, and your surroundings.

Are you unkind to that believing part of you? Sure! Just remember a bad day. Wham-o! Everything's shot to hell and that poor, precious, tender-loving part within you is riddled with psychological bullet holes and arrows.

Then your angels or God or your earth-bound angel friends have to march in and tidy up the mess. *And what a mess you do create within yourself!* You throw everything out with the bath water—baby, love, security, confidence—or all that sustains you throughout your trying days.

Well, this is not too big of a job for us angels, as we're Johnny on the spot. We just bring our heavenly mops, buckets, God's glue, and all our warm, woolly lovings [sic], and mop up the unearthly mess that you made of yourself, your life, and your surroundings.

And, of course, once you recognize our clean-up skills, you begin again to believe in us and the possibilities that we provide for you. You see, without your believing in angels from heaven or real ones living here on earth, you cut that lovely communication cord.

And that cord is our transmitting device. But once you see that that cord is again repaired with love and caring and a heavenly mop-up, you realize what you've done.

The simplest thing that you can do for yourself and for all of us heavenly beings is to throw away that 1% of doubt within your heart and mind and just give us 100% of your believing power and let us be your magical believing. We're far better at it than you are, for now.

Then each day your magic of believing will grow and grow. And very, very soon you will be a 100% believer in the possibility and the guarantee of our beloved, heavenly magic. It's a guarantee; it's more than a possibility!

And then you will know the truth of the magic of being a believer. And, thus, no more can your doubt creep in and destroy your pretty mind, body, and especially your oh, so delicate, fragile heart.

Then the magic of believing will result in a heart of different colors, all better and more glorious than a man-made hue. And this is the heavenly color of the magic of believing.

THE MAGIC OF BIG AND LITTLE MIRACLES

(**Author's note:** Being a survivor is a miracle in and of itself. Knowing that something special is happening to you and your family is beyond magic. If you are lucky, you will be present when the angels come to take your loved one home or when they come to simply have a conversation with him. When he speaks to you, listen to his unusual words. When you are in the room with him, notice the temperature and how it changes. And also be aware of all the changes within your relationship. All of these things are miracles that are happening. And they are more than earthly magic.)

Death is nothing but pure magic. How can you not see this? How can you avoid the things that are surrounding you? Quite easily my friend. The answer is that at this moment you are a part of every miracle. And right now everything that has happened between your birth and your loved one's death is rapidly entering your heart and mind.

In addition, each moment that you can spend with your loved one is so precious and is a miracle, too. This, in and of itself, should be totally blowing your mind and all your other senses. Too much magic always does this to human beings. I like to refer to this as angelic or heavenly overload.

Only when you too become an angel can you begin to see from a distance all the magic in each and every second of your time on earth. Right now you are more than likely feeling a sense of overkill from all the death-related events. And only God and I truly know how you are getting through the miracle of each day.

Miracles are happening all around and all the time. For instance, the magic of this moment. What is a moment? It is nothing. There is nothing here. And nothing is being lost. In addition, nothing is being gained. All of this is a miracle of space and breathing and me. It's just a time for you and me.

Well, this is how it seems to me; but remember I am viewing all of this from a distance and only through my angel eyes. Does this make my senses and my vision more acute than yours? By all means!

Now is the time for you to realize that little miracles bring new and different gifts, hopes, and loves. Are they less significant? Of course not! But you are not to worry, because if you miss the small happenings at this point in time, I will be back again tomorrow with something to make you see the importance of just a tiny miracle. After all, I have lots of time to love you and to show you the unobvious or the hidden meanings of your life.

I see change as a miracle. A little change is a little miracle. A big change is a huge miracle. And change is just a new miracle that is giving you a new gift. See it, touch it, hold it, and hug it tightly. And when you do this then the magic becomes you.

So, in your future, I see the magic of changes. No, they will not always feel loving and helpful. But, then again, neither did the process of your birth. And this is all as it should be.

The magic within all miracles is the knowledge that love and hope and peace are being conveyed to you. And that you receive all of this will show up in your eyes, through your smile, and in your capacity to love again. Let me help you find the magic that is in everything and everybody.

THE MAGIC OF COMING HOME

(**Author's note:** Simple things like going to the grocery store and then returning to your home may evoke different emotions. And these feelings will take on proportions that you are unfamiliar with. When this happens, you will know that more magic is entering your life, in a new and different way. When you can see this as magic, then you can begin to see your life as something to look forward to.)

Coming home has always had a glorious connotation, something like the anticipation of a great event; for example, leaving on that jet plane and traveling to some foreign spot. But coming home, on the other hand, is a more serene event, and one that has a different kind of anticipation.

Coming home refers more to a regrouping of your mind, body, and spirit in a known locale. It is a time of seeing the same old things but with a different twist. The eyes that you carried out the door of your house are not the same pair of eyes that return to your physical home. Your eyes have forever been changed during the time that you were away.

The eyes of the person who left your house saw only what he had experienced up to that point in time. They had known and digested the past information. Now upon your return to your home, you have seen more of your world and ours and now have more wisdom of the ages.

You see, your eyes are that part of your spirit that photographs things. During that process, they take in information; but they have no skills to decode that for you. They just snap pictures. They are intrigued by details, colors, and images. And so your eyes record this information that will then be processed by your brain and your heart.

Anytime that your heart gets involved with information that's when the knowledge becomes a bit garbled. That's because your heart is way too soft, sensitive, and endearing. All of your intake of beauty and wonderment then goes through all sorts of filters within your physical body and then later your glorious spirit and soul come into play, too.

Can you now begin to see that all that your eyes have taken in during your time away from home becomes more jumbled the closer you get to your house? Not only are your old responsibilities looming, but then there are all your new learnings that are getting pushed aside. You then begin to see the dilemma of the eyes, the body, and the mind in your old life plus the new learnings that you are experiencing.

You need to know that during your absence from home you have been collecting new pieces for your jigsaw puzzle that is called your life. This life then becomes more expanded, as somehow you have to find a location in that giant puzzle that you are now reconstructing. Sometimes the new pieces are not corner ones with distinct borders. Sometimes the pieces are odd shapes, and they aren't meant to fit at this point in time.

Those are the pieces that you leave on the edge of your so-called jigsaw puzzle of life and must wait a period of time for them to have a permanent resting place. Obviously, some of the colors in those puzzle pieces just ain't going to fit anywhere—maybe no time; no how. Then you must decide whether they should be discarded or merely cherished for what they were, but never make them a permanent part of your life puzzle.

Next time that you are driving home and are approaching your physical house—rounding each curve and corner in the road—notice that your eyes, your body, and your mind are playing a HUGE find-where-I-fit game with you. Realize that this is a beautiful process of fitting, of adjusting, and of absorbing all that has happened since you last pulled out of your driveway.

Your journey, to wherever you went, has caused your entire life to change in some way. Each turn of your car wheels or of your bicycle tires, every step of your pleasant walk or run, every single thing that you did and experienced has profoundly changed your puzzle of life.

Each of these has been a gift from God. Each of these was meant to happen. Each of these has been a miracle and such magic has been accomplished—all of which you are probably unaware.

If that hasn't all been magical, then the process of coming home certainly will be. Just expect magic to happen every moment of this period of time and returning will then become the magical gift of coming home to relish your newly-found treasures—the gifts of me to you.

I am the magic of your coming home. I am the magic within your mind. I am your magical puzzle of life. I will always help you to fit the pieces together. Please let me help you!

THE MAGIC OF DEATH

(**Author's note:** If you could see heaven and at the same time see your life on earth, your picture of the hereafter would be instantaneously changed. Your dreams for this lifetime would be immensely altered, enhanced, and be well received. Why does it always take a loved one's death to awaken you to your real life and to your most important task on earth?)

Death—hmmm, now that is an interesting word! Wonder where it really came from? Must have been something that God talked about, and then the word, death, was misinterpreted by man. Otherwise, it wouldn't cause so much pain and sorrow. I am sure that you know by now that God **never** makes up words that will be painful for his beloved friends like you.

Just what does death really mean? It means that a new drama is about to develop in your life. And it is a drama of proportions that you cannot possibly conceive of. It's a theatrical production to end all. It's a play that has been going on for eons, but one that is not visible from Mother Earth.

The scene has been the same for many centuries. What I can see is a life that all should long for, a drama of the universe. Where is this production being held? It's being held everywhere and should be a sell-out.

The best part of death is that it is a perfect time in your life. This is *never* a time of sorrow. This is never a thing to dread. This has always been a longed for and an ultimate gift from God.

This is a gift that is given to all. It is a gift of such permanence that it would make your head swim. It is a gift of love and hope and peace and growth.

"If God gives life and then also includes death in your dream for your life, then both of these events must be incredibly powerful, productive, and eye opening. The drama is yours to experience, to behold, and to cherish. So, why don't you do this?"

It must be that you on earth don't feel as though you have requested, written, and are truly a part of your own production that is called your life. If you did, you would realize that you are the only character in your own personal dream. You would know that the other actors, players, and loved ones are simply in your life to accentuate your ever being.

Of course, none of you are being paid in a monetary sense for your roles in your dream. You have all requested to be a part of this play, movie script—whatever you want to call it. You have all agreed to learn and to grow and to experience each other—with all your faults, attributes, quirks, lovings, longings, and heartaches. All of these things make each of you special, unique, and so valuable to the universe.

You have all shown up and been there for each other, in whatever sense that was required. You have all shared in each other's specialness. You have all given and taken, and always in the proper amounts, too.

You have all walked in and out of each other's lives. You have all held on, let go, and walked off stage on cue. Now, the moment of death will reunite you all in a new and better and more-highly-rated drama in heaven.

Sometimes you have altered the heavenly script to suit your wants and needs. Sometimes those alterations haven't been pleasant for you. At other times, they have been far superior. In all cases, the drama went on and was played out according to the dream for your life.

This is simply what has now happened. Your loved one's dream for his life on earth has ended, and that individual has now gone on to another dimension and is reunited with loved ones in heaven. This person has simply been written out of your life's dream. And thus this character is no longer in your personal drama here on earth.

Through whatever earthly feelings that you think you should have, need to experience, and are required to work through, you will continue with your life's dream. All that's different is that a person is missing. As a result, a new line is being written for your life; and another character may emerge. And thus another event is about to take place.

In all cases, your dream is still in the production stage. You are going on with new folks, events, and feelings. And new turns and twists will develop. This is the magic of your production of death. And it is one that is still being acted out and constantly altered in a perfect manner.

Nothing is unusual. Nothing has happened by chance. Nothing is going to destroy you and your life's dream. *Nothing is out of line!* It's just the magic of death and how you live it, love it, experience it, and want it to be written <u>and always just for you</u>.

THE MAGIC OF DEATH IS THE MAGIC OF LIFE

(**Author's note:** Your first recollection of death and heaven are your best memories, ones that will get you through this lifetime. Never look to other humans to explain what you know to be true. Live and breathe your own brand of magic and know that what is there is truly there for you.)

Death and all its magic is just the same stuff that God has bestowed upon your living. Nothing more; nothing less. Just plain magic.

You say that your life and all its foibles have to be much more complicated than magic? Go ahead and think that way. I'll wait . . .until those thoughts either do you in or reverse themselves and become much more hopeful and realistic in my terms.

So . . . I'm still waiting. Angels do this a lot, you know. You remember your mother describing this as having the patience of Job. You did not understand that cliché then nor do you want to comprehend it now.

What you've been given today in the way of gifts is simply and most easily understood in terms of magic. When you do this, the hard spots become smoother. The lumps become feather-like. The joys become higher and greater. The tears become less and more golden. And all of this for a reason—and most especially for your benefit, your joy, and your livelihood.

How you were conceived, now wasn't that truly magical, especially when you go beyond the biological aspects that you've learned in school? Wasn't it just a lovely magical chance that you became just you with all your pluses and your earthly-imposed minuses?

Wasn't this just as likely to happen as another glorious sunset or that beautiful moonbeam or how about your outrageous human giggle? Wasn't the joining of two human gene pools just as spectacular as a magician's wand? And the dust of the magic was sprinkled in the right places to create a spectacular <u>you</u>.

And when the dust of life's magic settled in different corners of your life, you realized that your time on earth was meant to be difficult. Something like no gain without pain. Something like needing rain before the sunshine. Something like waiting for your ship to come in. From where, I ask? Where and from whom these sayings emerged, that's what I'd like to know.

God has never been vague in his communication with his loved ones. He has never seen fit to communicate with you in a disorderly fashion. He would never think about wasting your time with words that weren't loving, caring, and giving. So, soon after your arrival on earth, you knew that you were lost and alone.

You discovered that life's dust became more like mud and bricks and boulders and walls to be climbed. The magic didn't seem to appear too often, if at all. The simple, lovely magic that you were born with and were told to weave into your daily life became an ironclad coat of not too many pretty colors. Not meant to be this way.

God's magic was intended to always be a major and <u>the most important part</u> of your lovely days. Unfortunately, man seems to have erased your magic, covered over your glorious colors, and buried you in muck and mire.

Remember your earliest knowings [sic] about death? Remember those memories that you brought with you into this life? Remember knowing that death was definitely a haven for your mind? Remember how bewildered you were to see your loved ones grieving for that first favorite person of yours who died when you were tiny and wise and still in tune with us?

Remember, and then keep remembering farther back and even much farther. The peace that you felt when your uncle died; the joyfulness that you so wisely knew was now his for eternity; the love you knew that was waiting for him on our side of the pond. Yes, I can see by your tears that you are remembering now.

At that point in time, your parents and other loved ones were beside themselves with grief. You were gleeful and playful, because you truly knew and could remember what awaited him. You see, three-year-olds have much finer minds than any older person can begin to imagine.

Your days were spent with your precious thoughts of God and angels and heaven and love. You wasted no time in grieving, because your knowings [sic] kept you more Godlike than any human knew. You had no tears, because no tears were needed. And without tears there is only perfect communication with God and me.

You knew no pain, as there was no need for it. You knew no sorrow, as there was only that magic that you so well remembered from the other side. You knew only truth and all of its reality. This is the magic of death, and the magic that God meant you to remember. The magic of me!

Now as an adult I have had to help you recapture your known magic of yesteryear. The magic of a tiny child! The magic of God! And all of God's magic of life and death that are simple, direct, and divine.

Is it more than simple magic? If it is, then I never want to know it, as I will never be able to comprehend it. And if I can't do this, then how could an angel or even God ever teach it to you?

The magic of life and death are the simplest moments of beauty, peace, joy, and the joining-togethers [sic] to see that world without end. See the sun? You see no end. See the sky. It never ends. See me? I, too, never end and neither will you.

A world of you and me together is what I give you—magic without end. See the magic! Know no end!

THE MAGIC OF EVERYTHING

(**Author's note:** You can be anything that you want to be. You can be a realist, a factual person. You can be a dreamer and believe in angels. You can be just a highly imaginative person who sees and hears things that others do not. You can be even more than all of these by believing in the magic that is in everything.)

Well, finally you have realized something that is very important. At last and for all time, you have become fully aware that your whole world operates on Magic Frequency 101 and not on some pre-destined, man-provoked system of occurrences. Now doesn't your life look like something that just might be fun and playful and productive, too? Magic, hum.

In a sense, you have now learned to love death. You just as well get use to this concept, as you have mini-deaths each and every day. And if you look at these events in this manner, you will eventually come around to the idea that all of these losses, challenges, and changes do prepare you for the real deaths in your life.

And, yes, you can lay extensive plans about the real deaths that are going to occur. You can have a list of supportive loved ones who hopefully will be there for you. You can have a list of helpful and affordable professionals, too. You can have a list of what people aren't suppose to spring on you and expect you to respond to—with dignity and grace (whatever that means).

And, yes, you can have your favorite list of things that you just ain't going to respond to. This list is entitled, "You Have a Right To Your Opinion about <u>Whatever</u>, and You Have A Right To Keep That Opinion To Yourself"—unless you want to set off a nuclear war. And this definitely includes things that aren't anyone else's business, personal stuff that is.

So what does this have to do with magic? Well, you do need all that is available in the universe to handle any change in your life. And you have just come through probably the worse event, the death of a loved one. And for you this lasted nearly 50 years or all of your adult life.

And during all of this time, you never thought that you had a husband, a family, a career, or friends who were magical. And you were right about this. But you were only right because none of those people were blatantly magical, heavenly, and angelic in appearance and manners. And you didn't know the right questions to ask about such powers and beliefs. Pity!

And now having lived through a stressful death and by chance asked for angelic help, you can see our handwriting on the wall or more explicitly on other humans. Now you can see and know when you are blessed. You look for angels in your daily life. And you go for broke in what you want from those angels. And, better still, God and I have seen you through this mess called your earthly life.

At last you can see the magic in everything that surrounds you. You can make magic out of things that you come in contact with. You can take the day and make it do what you want it to do. You have finally realized that the magic is you.

The magic's in everything that's seen and is about. It's touchable and yet vague. It's lovable and so dear. It's all about you and what you can see.

Now try and argue with me about these types of happenings:

The magic of the spirit of the darkness
The magic of morning
The magic of the darkness itself
The magic of the moment
The magic of your emotional waves
The magic of your destination

The magic of time
The magic of waste
The magic of space
The magic of freedom
The magic of me
The magic of the spirit
The magic of the light
The magic of the rain
The magic of change
The magic of its suddenness
The magic of others
The magic of that which is not seen
The magic of being in love
The magic of just being

All the world's a magic of some sort. It's the magic of being in love. And you can now see this. You can now be a part of that magic.

You are now all that you see. You are even more than me. The magic of everything is what God sent your way—not just for your first day but for every day.

You have earned it. How would you like to wear it? Let's go mix up a batch right now and share it with all that you see. Let the magic be all about me. Let the magic be all that you can be and see. Let the magic set you free.

THE MAGIC OF FATIGUE

(**Author's note:** The stressful fatigue that surrounds the dying process is only a symptom of where you are, what you were, and how you are going to be. There is nothing unusual about it, other than its playful presence. It plays on your mind, your body, and your spirit. It is the true essence of just how strong you now are and will have to be to experience tomorrow.)

Now, fatigue is an interesting word. Look at it. FAT-I-GUE! Ain't that pretty funny? See, already you're getting with the magic. Aren't I something else? Maybe your world should have more made-up words and more signs that all will be well in your life.

Whenever you quit laughing, we can go on with this magic. Look, it's already worked. And it is more magical than anyone can begin to comprehend. And that's what magic is.

Now you see that fatigue is really full of magic. What does this magic look like and feel like? The look is the smile on your face and the sparkle in your eyes. It is the sense that you will recover and will more than survive.

All of this is so very priceless that even God is smiling and nodding, and saying, "Yes, the magic of fatigue is so special and so precious. It's just too bad that everyone can't know this magic all the time. Life would be so much, more simple. *And I meant life to be simple and to be enjoyed—not all this stress and strife.*"

What's the feeling surrounding this magic? It's the fact that all other bodily senses disappear and that the overwhelming tiredness becomes most prominent. This is a holding-on device that keeps you with just one feeling and not a ton of others. This way your angels and spirit guides can come and hold you tightly and whisper words of encouragement in your ear and help you stay upright and safe and sane.

This holding-on device is one of someone else holding and caring for you during this awful time. These celestial folks will come and hold you and caress you and rock you to sleep each night. All you have to do is to ask for them to come and to protect you from your outside world.

Their service is free. The gift is *magnanimous*. The payoff is beauty. The time is now. The freedom is love. The way is easy.

The magic is simple. The fatigue is meant to be. The result is even more beauty and love and life for you—for forever.

THE MAGIC OF FEELING SHAKY

(**Author's note:** Some days your brain will only operate by making lists of things you are thinking, feeling, and need to do—even lists of nonsensical words. And don't be alarmed when your loved ones begin to label you and your lists as crazy. Not to worry, as the word, crazy, is right next to magic in God's heavenly dictionary.)

My word, you've made yet another list! Death does this to you. It encourages you to think in abstract, philosophical, and symbolic terms. But usually these are terms that no one else can comprehend, except me and your other angels and the universe. At such times, thank God for the universe.

Death tends to make you feel like a hot air balloon that has no place to land, no one to guide it, and no one that wants to observe its flight. Too bad you are unable to see its bright colors and its pretty lettering that says *"MEANT TO BE."* And then there are very few folks who are willing to clap profusely when your balloon lands safely. Too bad that death is such an erratic balloon ride that no one wants to buy a ticket.

This highly-personal balloon ride symbolizes your up-close experience with a magical transition, better known as your life in technicolor and operating at full speed ahead. Some of your feelings are due to:

The shakiness of your earth shifting
The shakiness of your sense of weightlessness
The shakiness of learning to fly anew
The shakiness of your personal sunbeams
The shakiness of all life
The shakiness of just shaking inside
The shakiness of a new love
The shakiness of a new life
The shakiness of loving again

The shakiness of losing your loved one
The shakiness of smiling
The shakiness of being whole
The shakiness of being invisible
The shakiness of a new reality
The shakiness of just shakiness

Well, there you have it—your very own list for today. It
means the world to you. It sends just the right message to us. And
who cares if no one has a clue about what you are talking about.
Just smile for you and for where you are, feeling really shaky.

Feeling this shakiness is a pretty common occurrence for
you. Most of your life you have felt this way. Most of your life has
been seen as something unexplainable, daunting, and downright
fearful. That is, until I came into your life to stay.

What's so special about having an angel living with you? I
can make you feel whole. I can bring you peace. And I can be there
at all times, through thick and thin, and at all hours of the day and
night. And at this most stressful time in your life, I am the angel to
bring you home and to explain God's world and reign to you.

Right now you are feeling so shaky, sort of like a bowl of
Jell-O and more fragile than you have ever felt before. Why
wouldn't you feel this? Death always shakes humans into another
state of being, sort of like a place halfway between heaven and
earth.

And your world is shaking from its center outward, too.
You are like that molten mass in a volcano when it turns liquid.
And right now you are very unstable. Too bad the local television
station won't come and film what is going on within you. They run
all around the world to get pictures of the next big volcanic blow.
Why not you?

To most folks, death is also the biggest earthquake imaginable. And, unfortunately, this quake gets no seismic reading and often comes without warning. No one records anything in the annals for posterity. Therefore, you never know just how shaky you are. And other well-meaning folks cannot be relied upon to tell just how you are faring and what your Richter scale would read. What a blessing it would be if some mortal would invent one of these gadgets for humans so that others could truly know and feel and understand your pain.

Your shakiness will depend upon your spiritual teachings and how your family coped with death. Unfortunately, none of these things are going to aid and assist you unless they taught you about the magic of you and the magic of death and the magic of the universe. Want a short course on all this magic?

The best magic in your shakiness is that no matter how bad it gets, we will always be there for you. You have no reason to worry, as we will never forsake you. We will never leave you to be alone with your fragile nature at this time in your life.

At no time will I be anything but a ray of sunshine for your sadness. And I can help you to find this same ray of hope within yourself. And if you let this beam of sunshine warm and cradle you, I can guarantee you that I will be able to guide and to love you and to be with you until your death.

You say that this guarantee is quite a huge one. You say that you wish that your entire life had been like this. You say that I am beyond belief. Well, I will first tell you that I ain't a spirit for nothing. And secondly I could not be a part of God's heavenly world if I did not tell you the truth and share his promise with you.

A promise made is a promise earned. When I came to be your angel who would stay with you until the moment of your death and at that point in time I would go with you into heaven, I made a promise to you that you had already earned.

You deserve this type of love and support. And once you knew that all you had to do was to ask for my heavenly assistance, you learned that all promises were meant to be kept. I simply made a promise to you, one that will never be broken—no matter what.

Now your world's finally awakening to a new and different you. You are a treasure to behold. You are a jewel waiting to be cut and polished. And it's a beauty that I love. You're my light, my sun, my sparkle—you're me! You will be me.

So what is this physical shaking that you are experiencing? I am simply shaking you so that you will come back to be with me and allow me to explain to you what is happening. And every time that you sense something new and different and terrifying, you immediately rush to your tablet to write or to your computer.

Thank God, you are not trying to fly away without me again and without wings, too. At least you are recording what is going on and allowing yourself to see it in print and to then use your intuition at a later date to put things right. Your journals and writings aren't just for you. They are for all of us to use to gauge your progress, your love, and your light within.

Have you even seen a shaky light? Well, that is what is going on with you. You know that that special spirit who glows within you is teetering on the edge of that volcano or near the fault line of that earthquake. Not to worry!

Guess who is gently and lovingly holding, nourishing, and guiding that light? Right! Me and your fleet of angels. Ever see a fleet of angels fall into a volcano or run from an earthquake? Not likely.

Just come back into our arms and let us hold you for a while. Soon you will be giggling again and alive and loving all of us. You are simply experiencing another way to come back home—to a home that you know so well, our arms and our world.

We are the magic of your shakiness. Thanks so much for recognizing our energy, our love, and our hope for you. And thanks, too, for the privilege of allowing us to hold and cradle you through all these feelings—all the feelings of universal love.

THE MAGIC OF FEELING
TICKLED AGAIN

(**Author's note:** Laughter heals and calms and makes you feel light and airy. Sometimes it is a part of your day, but more than likely it is missing. Best you find something to laugh about each day. Best you find a new feather and brush it across your skin so that you can once again feel that special tickling sensation. And then smile and let it consume you.)

I just bet that you're truly wondering if you'll ever bubble over again with laughter and great peals of giggles and merriment. I just bet that God is awaiting that day, too. He is going to be so happy to see that you can once again laugh until you cry and can hardly wait to race to the bathroom before you embarrass yourself before God and who knows else.

Remember those times in your life? Remember what that feeling was like? Remember when you literally wanted to roll on the floor and just continue laughing until you could hardly breath? Remember how it felt to be so childlike and free and full of it?

Well, my friend, that time is once again upon you. You've reached a stage where you can now make laughter happen at will. You no longer have to look for an amusing incident. You can now create them for yourself. Now is the time to find anything and everything amusing and giggle away your days. Now comes the freedom that also comes with death!

You all on earth have this morbid sense of your loved one being far away and gone and dead. This isn't like God's world at all. You have it all wrong; and, I'm here to tell you that you all have to shape up or else.

Of course, the "or else" is or else you're going to miss out on all the fun that God wants you to have for the rest of your life. Your life must be one of frivolity and dreams and giggles and feeling just downright tickled.

If you do not believe this, then I dare you to call up one of your loved ones and ask that person to come and tell you about his present life in heaven. There isn't anything that gives angels more fun than to see you doubled over with ridiculous, outrageous laughter at the dumbest thing that has happened in your day.

What do we do then? Of course, we dance and sing and clap for all your hard earned right to have fun and to see the beauty in the ridiculousness of your earthly days.

You've earned the right to rejoice in your own survival after the death of your loved one. Remember all those fancy words about celebrating life? Well, just what do you think God meant? He certainly didn't mean for any of the morbid happenings that I've seen since I've come to live with you.

You went from a fairly coping human being to a wallowing wonder. And it's a wonder that I even recognized you as even one of God's gifts to the world. My God! You have carried on for oh, so many days and nights and weeks and months and years. Do you have any idea how heavy you are to hold up 24 hours a day? Well, let me tell you.

Find the biggest pachyderm, the hughest [sic] building, the greatest dam that holds water—you know one of those concrete structures that just may hold back water for constructive purposes like irrigation and drinking. Find anything that's so heavy that no man could begin to hold up by himself. This is how heavy you've been for me. You've been a heavy burden to hold, and I've been very blessed to have been chosen to do this.

What would I be worth to you if I couldn't say how grateful I am to have been chosen to accompany you throughout the remainder of your life? And what a life it's going to be, too. A life like none other! A life you've always longed for! A life that I am blessed in helping to create. Does this sound like a burden to you? I think it's like a blessing for both you and me and obviously for the world, too.

You see your burden has now been turned into a new blessing, a blessing of hope and love and freedom. This freedom from all your pain now gives you new gifts, new visions, and new beings in your life.

Now the true magic of death can emerge. And it's the magic of the freedom to laugh and to go on and to be all that God meant you to be. And I can guarantee that I'm going to make that happen and so are you. It's my guarantee to you!

It's more than a possibility! It's the absolute guarantee of more laughter, more loves, more dreams, and more giggles. Now, you can truly smile about all the giggling that is coming your way. Do you mind if I help with the magical tickling?

THE MAGIC OF FLOATING

(**Author's note:** At the time of a death it is healthy to know that you will float through many days, weeks, and possibly years. Yes, you will be physically present; but mentally and spiritually God and your angels will come to carry you through. And being carried by heavenly beings means floating in time and space with the best folks.)

Floating, you say. What's that? Is it necessary at the time of a death? What on earth is it? Do I mean that now you can fly? Almost.

After a death, you'll find yourself just mentally drifting away. It is like your mind is a million miles away, but your body is definitely in the here-and-now. There's no doubt as to where you are physically—right here on planet earth with the bills, the responsibilities, the correspondence, the feelings that always surround a death, and with the knowledge that no way your life will ever be the same. Who wouldn't want to escape and run away from all of these?

Can all of these things be avoided? No. Can you decide when to float and when not to? No. Can you choose how and when and where this occurs? No, sir-re-bob!"

Nothing is a choice for you. Nothing is a given at any point in time. Nothing is what is given to you, and in the most delightful way.

It's like all the healing magic of the universe is given to you to use as a gift—whether or not you want it then and there. You see, sometimes magic is more than magic. Sometimes it's God's way of saying, "No, my dear, you can't look at another reality without the magical sawdust and moon dust and angel dust. Come let me hold your hand and walk with you."

Sometimes there's only one magnificent entity who can sustain you. You see, floating is being able to see beyond today. It's being able to be held by the most wonderful being in the universe. It's being loved so much and more than you can ever imagine in an earthly sense.

It's being taken into another's heart and being held there in suspension until you can once again regroup and come up with some way to cope on planet earth. See, it's <u>even much </u>better than chocolate candy.

How many times since your loved one has died have you wanted someone to hold you and to say soothing things to you? How many times did you want that someone to always be there for you on a continual basis, day in and day out and for all time? How many times have you longed to just be free of all that has transpired? How many times is one-many times [sic] too many?

To say that all of this will go away in a minute is to deceive you. To say that your pain and suffering will run its course is to try to fool you. To say that believing in me and in your other angels will be the trick is to lie to you. To say that one day you'll feel better is just inhumane to say to you.

So, you see, saying just sometimes won't do anything for you. Now those are the times that we're trying to catch up with you as you float away to be with God. Isn't it terribly special and important to know that when you are your worst that then that big, big person steps in to see you through?

Ask him for whatever you need and whenever and however you want it. Demand that your bucket be filled up. Tell him in whatever way possible just how horrible you are feeling and that you need relief <u>right now</u>. Demand that you be sustained with whatever you want and need. Don't settle for anything less.

And then when you have nothing more to ask for, you just might ask for all the love that you are missing. Because, you see, floating is an absence of love and not a sign that there is anything wrong with you. Your loving has just been diminished, and you need huge amounts of God's continual love to be there for you on call at any time of the day or night and for all times.

And once you know how that feels to be over loved and greatly, greatly appreciated for everything that you are and do, then you can ask for all those other things that you want, too. Don't forget to ask for those flying lessons. Or if you prefer to sail away in a ship, then maybe you best have lessons captaining.

Your love for him and what you are given in return are the real test of floating away on a sea of love. That sea is one that is eternal, bigger than the universe, and totally free of charge. Imagine, you can float for free and really and truly learn to be free, too. Hell of a deal!

THE MAGIC OF FORGETTING

(**Author's note:** Forgetting everything about your loved one is very unlikely. But this magic that your angels will bring to you is something to behold. It is a heavenly reorganization of your mind, your body, and your soul—and in such a more logical, mythical, spiritual way. Forgetting is really something that you want to experience. So ask and ye shall receive all the help that you need from the universe.)

A death, a loss, a change—they all tell you and say the same things. They tell you about pain and sorrow and loved ones going on before you. They tell you about you and me. And most of this, from your perspective, is uncomfortable, potentially devastating, and just plain hurtful.

So the death has occurred, and the devastation is massive. The tears flourish. The heartache seems to never end. Your life is in shambles—probably physically, definitely psychologically, and potentially economically, too. Changes always frighten you, and always will. Never again will you be exactly the same. And just ain't that a blessing?

Don't bother to answer, as I know what you're thinking, "This geek's off the wall and understanding nothing about me." Here you're totally wrong. How could I be talking to you as I do without having lived with similar pain and sorrow and deaths? No one knows you better than a fellow sufferer who's now your angel in disguise.

Time's gone by. Pieces have been assembled or discarded. Tears have diminished some. That scab on the hole in your heart and your life is sort of healed and stays somewhat in place, at least for longer periods of time. Every second doesn't seem like eternity and so full of sorrow. In fact, some things are really looking quite good. Sounds like it's time for forgetting.

Again I just know what you're thinking. Will you remember how your loved one looked, walked, talked, smiled, and giggled? Will you remember how special that person was to you? Will your memories be enough to sustain you until you two meet again? Will your life be enhanced or destroyed if you forget?

What will you forget that you're not even aware of? Will you forget the right things or the wrong things? Will forgetting mean that you'll love that person less? Will your love be constant and strong enough?

Will forgetting be more than forgetting? Will all this result in your moving farther away from that person instead of closer to that individual in heaven?

Heavy questions, you say. Damn heavy, painful questions I say. And questions are just that, questions, nothing more and nothing less. And just where would you be without magical questions?

Remember, I came to you as the result of all those sad and painful questions that you asked of the air in your house. Without those questions, we would not be together now. And even if it's not in a physical sense, it's a beautiful marriage of spirit and friend or angel on earth.

Questions are what I love the best about you. You ask. I reply. You grow. You go on with life. And I thrive here beside you and hold you up through all these new experiences. Ain't that a pretty picture and one that you really should paint for all the world to see?

Do you really remember every question that you've ever asked of God, another person, or of me? I truly doubt it. You see questions are just heavenly secrets that you long to know the answers to. Forgetting is much the same, but in a different way.

Now you're questioning once again if forgetting will make you thrive or throw you off balance. To forget is just what it says in that word. First, there's the word, for; and then there's the word, get. The word, for, means going toward something. And to get, very obviously means to enhance yourself and your life. Therefore, to forget means that something more important will replace your wonderings [sic].

If you forget the death and all its sordid details, you are simply now replacing that pain with new lovings, thoughts, lustings (if appropriate), dreams, hopes, and human angels. You are now experiencing the magic of forgetting or the magic of going forth.

Will I love you less if you do this? Will you remember less? Hell, no! All this means is that you will give me another earthly angel to guide, teach and love. When you let another new person or event into your life, you're simply giving me new and extended access to another earthly being.

When you add to your life, you also add to my experiences here in heaven. Really, you're simply going forth and getting more believers, more humans who care and love and need to know about us heavenly beings. When you get, then we get, too, and in even greater quantities than you do.

Go-for-to-get [sic] all that is rightfully yours and ours. The love will remain the same. The memories can always be excavated and revisited, if you really need to do that again. If not, then let all of us go on together and get all that God planned for you in your beautiful life.

Make us one. Make us work. Make us all a part of your forgetting and getting, too. We'll help you make this process of forgetting <u>even more</u> than just magic!

THE MAGIC OF FRIENDS

(**Author's note:** Friends are very important to a grieving person. What they say, how they say it, and when they deliver their concerns are all a part of one's recovery. Think twice before being overly blunt. Think more than twice before ever assuming that a survivor is actually and truly surviving. Let this call be hers and not yours. Ask for magic when in doubt.)

Friends make the magic of the world believable. They're those rare beings that have been sent into your life by God and all for very specific reasons and lovings [sic]. Reasons and lovings. I like the sound of that. Makes me think of dreams and mountains and peace and salvation. Makes me wonder if one ever sees all the blessings that God has given.

Dreams—friends are dreams come true. Ever remember how you truly longed for just that person who would come into your life to share your every thought and your ever being? That's a dream, and a true and loving friend can fulfill that place in your heart for all times. Isn't that a pretty thought? Someone to be near and dear and true, always.

This person is truly a gift to you. This individual loves you no matter how much of a fool you make of yourself. This person is simply a gift given on the wind and one that will blow and go with you wherever God directs his wind to send you.

This person is really a gift at the time of your loved one's death. That's the first person that you reach out to with every gory detail and every blessed moment of hope. That's the person that you ring up in the night and cry your heart out to. That's the person that always seems to be home at just that moment and says, "I'm here for you no matter what. Not to worry."

That's the person who tolerates all your bizarre and ungracious thoughts and doesn't tell you that you're a damn fool. That's the person that enfolds you and your strifes into such big loving arms and says, "You know that you and your problems are always welcome in my life. I'll always make time for you." Is that a gift or what?

The gift you are! Yes, you, too, are a gift to your friend. You're the gift of learning. You're the gift of hope. You and your problems are the gift of hope for the future. You see all your joys and sorrows are gifts to both of you.

How is that magic? All things happen for a reason. All reasons are for learning. All of this sounds like something that is inconceivable to the earthly mind. This is magic! This is the magic of friends.

THE MAGIC OF GOD RETURNING FROM HIS HOLIDAY

(**Author's note:** Before and after a death, the survivor may question God's existence, his presence, and just where he has been. Perhaps he hasn't answered your prayers in a timely fashion. Perhaps he seems too far away to reach. Perhaps he's more than you can imagine and one whose presence is just assumed. And all of this is true. Why?)

So, you think that God's been on a holiday? Seems to be what you've been feeling. Seems to be that's how it's looked from where you are and have been. Seems to be that's how you've been feeling and thinking. Seems to be how it's been for you. Seems to be the color of your world lately. Maybe it's just seemed to be that way!

Maybe we need to first talk about God and his life. Maybe you need to understand that his world is really magnificent. Maybe you need to realize that his vantage point is one to really behold. Maybe it's time for you to know.

Let's start with his home. What would you picture it to be? Would you imagine a huge white mansion on a hill? Would you think it was a palatial domain? Would you want it to be greater than the house that you live in? Would you really even be able to envision it if I told you?

Maybe you should try this on for size. Maybe you should just imagine the most beautiful home that's filled totally with love and colors that aren't of your world on earth.

Maybe you should paint that picture for yourself in your own mind, as it is all of these and even more and so, so pretty and serene.Maybe the mansion that he lives in is more important in your mind than in his. He lives in such a place, and he owns everything in your world that you somehow imagine that you possess. Ironically, you're just a caretaker for all that he owns in your life. You own nothing; he owns everything in your world.

The mansion that he lives in is within your mind right now. That's just the prettiest thing that he has ever created for you. You are the mansion that he lives in all the time. He is you. And you are him. There's no separation and no way to separate the two of you.

So where does he go on vacation or holiday? He comes to share that time with you. He comes to give you a treat beyond belief. He doesn't come to eat off of you, as no food is needed for this special guest. There are no clothes to be washed, no beds to be made, and no trouble having him as a guest in your home.

He comes to share in your day and asks only that you entertain him while he's on holiday with you. He's there when you have problems with your car. He's there in your dreams each night. He's there in your gleeful times. He's there in your sorrow and sadness. He's just there with you while you think that he's on holiday somewhere else in the universe.

Holiday to God means being with his most beloved creature that he's created—you. God's best holiday is being with you in your mind, your heart, your being. His greatest and most sought-after holiday is just spending time with you.

Just when you think that he's gone from your life, that's the time to look around and know that he's packed his bags (so to speak) and has come to spend time with you in your days, in your dreams, and in your life. He knows when to come. He knows how long that he can stay. He knows when to step back and to not get too close. He knows when all is well with you. And he knows when his holiday with you is over and when you can operate with just your memory of his time with you.

How do you know that he's there? Look around—sense, see, and remember those times that you felt that you weren't alone. Remember those times when something was out of place in your life. Remember those times when something blew up and needed to be repaired in your home, your car, your life. Remember when and how you felt just then. Well, that's when you know that he's there.

God is on holiday all the time! Don't you get the picture? It's his world. Everything belongs to him. Everything has a purpose and a reason. Everything is where he is all the time; he made it. He shares in it. He guards over it. And he's there always vigilant and watching and caring and giving you signs.

If you think that he's on holiday and not with you, you best look around. He's everywhere, all at the same time. He's never far away.

No! He doesn't sleep. No! He's not ignoring you. No, he's never packed his bags and gone elsewhere. You're the one that packs your bags and goes on a trip and thinks that you're escaping him. Do you really think that he's not in the car with you? Think again, my friend.

Holiday means holi-day. Get the picture—holy day? How can you have a day without him when each day is a holi-day. You're the one that's on holiday with him, and you don't even know it. Well, now you do.

You are God's holiday, and that's every day for you. He loves nothing more than spending time with you. He loves being in your every dream and wish and joy and sorrow. When will you join him in his holiday called your life?

All of this is hocus-pocus, you say. Not! You are the magic within God's holiday, which is every day of your life. The magic is you. You are the magic of his holiday. Bet you don't know how magical this is. I do! And now you know, too.

THE MAGIC OF GOING ON WITH YOUR LIFE

(**Author's note:** When you hear the phrase, going on, from someone else, it means something entirely different than if you yourself are saying it. The phrase needs to be seen in a magical sense, one that will give you peace, hope, and some salvation. Without this meaning, it carries the connotation of drudgery, sadness, and strife. It definitely needs to be seen as a you-and-me-together activity, or one of angel togetherness.)

Will you ever know when it's the right time to go on with your life? No! Going on means so many things that you're probably not aware that you're even doing it. You see, going on is really doing everything at once, not being aware that this is happening, and then later realizing that going on has truly occurred.

More than likely if you conjure up a game plan about going on with your life, you're going to miss the whole experience. You are never to know what this is suppose to mean for you and your life nor are you to know specifically when it is to happen. It's sort of like magic.

No human heart can ever engineer the magic of going on. There's no way that even I can teach you what it's all about. It is just one of those magical, miracle-type things that suddenly happen, and all in good time, and for each person in a very unique and special way.

For you, even saying the words, going on, brings such huge tears to your eyes and such racking sobs. I hate to see this reaction, but it is a necessary one. And it is one that you do know so well, but have long forgotten or else stored away within a special place inside your heart.

The process of going on is similar to a gentle ocean wave, just a gentle lapping of the water at the edge of the shoreline. It's not a huge erosive wave that encompasses you.

It's the ever, so gentle shifting of those fine granules of sand. They're just lovingly being moved from one location to another. Of course, they're never destroyed, just being rearranged for a prettier and more beautiful effect, especially for you and your life.

Your whole life has been about going on, from babyhood to adolescence to adulthood. Haven't you really been going on whether you wanted to or not? Did anyone ever ask you if you really wanted to give up those diapers? Hell, no! Someone thought that it was way past time for you to be potty trained.

All of life is like this, someone else knowing what is probably going to be the best for you and when you should go on and live your life. At least now you're laughing at the prospect of going on with your life.

In actuality, all of your life has been one of constant and foreboding changes and going on. Have you ever gotten up one morning and said, "Self, do you really want to go on with today?" I doubt it. And the process of getting on with your life after the death of your loved one happens in just this same way.

Going on simply means holding your head up a little higher. It means knowing that the tears will still come, but that now each tear means something new and brighter. It no longer is that gut-wrenching sobbing about anything and everything. Most times, you can now identify something that has provoked your tears. This is going on.

Going on is also knowing that the love of your life is truly never coming back, but that each day that individual has more firmly implanted himself within your heart and soul. Now you do know that he walks with you and talks with you and from the inside of you out. He is not that angel that just hovers about you, but he is deep within every part of you and always and forever will be there.

That very special angel power that is now yours is always accessible. You don't have to ever call him up. He is a part of your speaking, your hearing, and your feelings—just part of everything about you. You obviously aren't always aware of this, but every now and then you will catch yourself and think, "Oh, I know where that thought or feeling is coming from."

It is truly like being one with each other, for always and forever and for all times. It is the you and me together and not just when you want it to be true, but at all times and for all time. Come and let me take your hand and walk with you and help you to go on with your life. We're going to have a lot of fun together.

Believe me! Life is fun. Life is magic. You and me together can make more magic come true than just one of us acting and standing alone. Take my hand and say that you will follow me. And I will do the same for you. Look at your hand and know that I am within it. Your hand and mine are one and the same, all of it magic. Let's go make it all come true.

THE MAGIC OF GOOD-BYES
AND NOT
BEING ALONE

(**Author's note:** How do you envision yourself being alone? Your loved one will come at a moment's notice to help you through the rough spots and also celebrate your great moments, too. Is this really being alone or is it simply believing in a magical person who is now with you 24-7? Death does make the spirit world more up close and personal and even more loving. They have far more magic to weave for you than you do as just one human being.)

I just bet that you have anguished over saying good-bye to your loved one. I bet you don't like the sound of the word, good-bye. I just bet that you think that it's a daunting task.

I can just hear you saying, "I'm not ready to do this." Or "I just can't do that now." I can just hear every excuse in the book to put off this task and to not face your own future and your endless possibilities of success and love and dreams.

I can also just imagine that you're wondering how this can be an act of magic. The world is all about magic and nothing else. If you don't think that God and angels and spirits are magical, then we need to have a really serious talk. Cause I'm telling you that God does want to be thought of in these terms and with the amount of hope and dreams that the word, magic, conjures up in your mind. Talk about the ultimate dreamer . . . . hmmmm.

When you say good-bye to your loved one, just whom are you going to be talking to? Why that person, of course. Therefore, the first thing that you want to do is to call up that angel, that spirit, that entity, and talk directly to the person.

Why say all this stuff to someone else? Why not go right to the source, and do the job up right in the beginning? It's easy! And it's the only sensible way to do it.

Do you have any idea what this will do for that person's spirit? Do you or can you even begin to imagine how glorious it is to hear your name called from somewhere in the universe? Do you know what special meaning that has for your loved one?

Yes, I guess from the tears in your eyes that you are now making the connection and realizing how precious it is to have a call from home. Yes, us angels do want and need to hear from you earthlings. Yes, we want to help to ease your pain in every way. Yes! Yes! We will come. Yes! We want to be there for you. Just try us; you are going to like having us around.

Simply say your loved one's name out loud and ask the person to come and to be with you in your home. Then begin to pour your guts out—all the uglies [sic] that need to be said plus all the glorious words of love and of hope, as well as of longing and of dreams.

Don't forget that angels can take anything that you dish out to them. They process it in the right vein. They know exactly what you're saying when even you don't know what you're trying to convey. They truly know your gut-wrenching fears, doubts, and frustrations.

No matter what you say, they will always love you unconditionally and at all times and everywhere that you may go. They are always near, and you are never ever alone.

Keep talking, crying, railing, and loving—whatever it takes for you to work through your grief so that you can go on with your life. You call this grief. I call this loving your child, your friend, your lover, or your relative to death.

Hey, we can handle this. Your grief is just a continuation of your loving process. We just use different terms to say the same things.

Good-byes are just more lovings [sic], and your world certainly needs much more of this. So keep talking to your loved one—out loud, remember. The person will come, will listen, and will respond.

And don't be at all surprised when he gives you answers that you have never thought of and wonderful solutions to what is troubling you. Go to the source of your pain, and there you will find your greatest joy. Love it; hold it; converse with it, and it will bring you peace.

MAGIC OF HEALING

(**Author's note:** Healing is an ever moving target, and one that truly does not exist. When you are healed, do call me. Then you can personally tell me what is true for you and wherein your magic lies. And magic is the beauty that you find within yourself to love and laugh again. I want to see and feel the magic, too.)

Healing? Do you really and truly believe that there is such a concept that exists? Does it make any sense to you that you'll ever get over some of your losses? Who came up with such a word that would denote that all was once again well and safe and secure and the same? Sounds like another one of your earthly dictionary words that probably makes absolutely no sense to most humans but that many will hesitate to argue with.

Why don't you on earth voice your opinions more about things that hurt you so deeply. For example, how about the healing words and things that just point out to you that you are suppose to do this or that in order to be normal? Or the authorities that tell you that you are to follow some path and go down it in an orderly fashion. Then you are to pop out on the other side of the rat maze that is called your life. And, how dare anyone tell you that you are to do this right on schedule and with all of your body and mind perfectly intact. Isn't there something out of place in this description?

Healing might mean that you have a scab that has pretty much covered over your exposed and terribly painful wound from your loved one's death. The scab will more than likely come off—eventually; but what about that scar underneath? Is that wound totally and forever healed? Or are you really supposed to think this?

If it was a terribly deep wound, then the scar is going to be extraordinarily sensitive for years, maybe decades, and maybe for your entire life. When is this healed over? Or is it ever?

To other folks, when you stop endlessly talking about your loved one that is when you are healed. What sense does that make? Shutting up is simply putting up with what society wants you to do. This definitely ain't being healed. If anything, it is simply creating an endlessly deep, sorrowful wound that will always be present, will always hurt, and will always keep you on the brink of extinction—the extinction of you.

Healing isn't the big things that you do. Healing is the small, tiny baby steps that make you move. Healing may be something as simple as a tiny smile that eases your mind and heart for just a second. Healing isn't anything like a huge celebration to mark the end of your grief.

If you believe that death is pretty mythical, then you must also believe that healing is a total myth. How can anyone analyze this when it cannot be seen, touched, held, and loved? It's a pretty magical experience and an extremely personal one at that.

Try and find anyone with a similar death experience as yours with exact events, feelings, and outcomes. Then tell me truthfully if you would even believe what that person tries to tell you. I doubt it.

Healing happens or it does not happen. It depends upon your script for this lifetime and upon how much your powerful free will has intervened and altered events and reactions. Whatever you throw out into the universe, so does it come back to you. The same holds true for healing, as your reaction is so automatic.

Therefore, whatever is in your script that was decided upon in heaven before you came back to earth is how your life and your feelings will evolve. Everything is sown and then reaped or given and always received according to plan, your individual life plan.

Don't ever look for healing or expect it in major, major loss situations. If you don't believe me, then try to tell a parent that he will heal after the death of a child. Then throw into that equation the fact that the parent is ultra sensitive. And to make it even more complicated, throw into the pot the fact that the parent is psychic.

Or the fact may be that the parent has never, ever dealt well with death and God and recovering.

Or perhaps the child's death was never dealt with in any fashion and consequently the parents' marriage has ended in divorce. Then there are other children's feelings to consider, as well as the grandparents'. With so many factors, I think you are getting the picture that healing is a never-to-happen event. A muddling through life and an appearing to cope is the most that anyone should expect with most deaths.

Therefore, the magic of healing is only that tiny fraction of a minute when you feel better after a death. Or it might be that little giggle that erupts deep down inside of you while watching a television show. Or it may be finding that certain foods once again taste good to you or it might simply be the fact that you have enough energy to get out of bed in the morning and decide that you might like to eat. Little things are healers.

You see, healing is simply being able to recognize the life that is still within you. It is telling yourself (and hopefully making yourself somewhat believe it) that you need to stand up and move in some direction, even if it is not in a forward direction. I think that it's simply called "move it." And sometimes this takes every ounce of energy that you possess.

You make up the rules on grieving, on standing up, and on healing. And therein lies the magic. Unless you make up the magic and keep making it up and make it all extremely personal, you will never find it or feel it or be able to live until you die.

If this means asking your loved one to come back and be your angel-in-waiting or guardian angel, then do this. No matter how bizarre or how farfetched you have to become to go on living, then just plan on doing that. Now, it might be advisable to tell your friends and loved ones that you are doing this, as you have no better way to survive.

Whatever it takes to survive and to find the magic, then just plan on doing that. Only when you ask your angels for the magic will you receive it. You see we hate to butt in and be rejected. Esteem, you know. Angel ego, too.

Just know that we will never fail you and will serve you perfectly. And, most of all, we want you to know and realize our presence and our 24-hour-a-day loving and guiding that we can and will give to you.

Ask, demand, whine—do anything! Just get our attention and ask for more magic so that you can write your own book on healing. Magic that will lead you to some semblance of life without your loved one. If you create it, it will serve you well. Then the magic is truly you!

THE MAGIC OF HOME

(**Author's note:** Home is truly your way of being. It is a sense of your wisdom, your experience, and your need to be real. And death does make the survivor more real. There no longer is that place to hide with that loved one. Now you are your own psychological house within a familiar and yet very different person.)

Home! What a peaceful, joyful place. What a haven for the mind. What a place of salvation. What a love to anticipate. What a place. What a time I'm going to have. Home! Yes!

Haven't you always felt this way at the thought of going home to where you live? Isn't that the feeling that you have as you turn that last corner on your block or that last bend in the road before you can actually see that structure that you call home?

Can't you just picture your house in your mind and what's there and the folks that will welcome you? Don't you just feel that love welling up in your heart and those funny drops of excitement going all over your body? I always did. I sure hope that you do, too.

Home means many things to folks. Home is sometimes depicted as being where your heart is. That means that wherever you wander that you always carry your heart and your home with you. This is true. Without this feeling of being at home within your own body and mind, I doubt that you could function throughout your life. This home is a mobile one, and one that is really the shell of your person and contains all your vital working parts. This is a really vital home for you to carry around.

Then there's the physical home that you live in. This is constructed from manmade materials and houses all your worldly material goods. You know, those things that you tell yourself that you can't live without. Those things that you pick up at the store and drag home to clutter up your premises. Bet you all have done just that.

Stuff! That's what is really housed in this home. Stuff that someone may want after you die, and stuff that more than likely no one is ever going to want except you. This stuff is what makes a house a home. It's a reflection of you and who you are and what you may hope to be one day. Stuff makes the house a home.

Within this physical home, you hopefully have a loved one living there with you. A somebody that you would lay down your life for! A person that you can hardly function without. A person that is your one-and-only lover. A person who is your dream of a mate. A person that you'll love for forever. Just a being that will always live in your heart and share your physical home with you.

Can't you just picture that person or persons who share your home? Can't you almost reach out and touch them in your mind? Can't you just sense their presence and their touch on your body? Isn't this just the home that you've always longed for? Aren't you looking for this?

And now that a death has occurred, you need to reevaluate who you are, where you live, and what you want that place to look like. It probably will be a different color, have a new aura about it, and even be in a more luxurious setting.

And all of these new looks will be who you are by yourself. If you know all the answers, then the process has already been done. But home more than likely will be a new vista, a new being, a new person in your life.

Yes, a house can be like another human being. One that holds you, guards you, and lets you be yourself. And you definitely want one that is more than you thought it would ever be. If you think big, then your house will project a bigness to you and to your world. All it has to do is present you with the confidence and the joy and the peace that you long for.

All the love and tending that you put into your home will then be projected back into your life. For all it costs and all it's worth, your house will be your security blanket to a new and more lovely you. It will help to make you into the being who now stands alone and within the magic known as herself.

THE MAGIC OF HOPE

(**Author's note:** Hope is truly a gift from God. It might be manmade, but more than likely it won't work as well as God's. Why? Because when you ask for gifts from another dimension you get way more than what you're familiar with on earth. Unseen magic and angels and dreams—these are what you'll get. These are the things you need to build a newer you.)

It's a feeling like none other. It's such an explosiveness that it's often unidentifiable and goes undetected. Hope's not a feeling of joy, as most think. It's a dynamic compilation all its own. Notice that you truly don't know what I've just said or described. That's hope.

This hope of yours is all that is beyond you. It's a feeling of peace, joy, sadness, trauma, fear, and not knowing. Once it's all rolled up into one, it becomes an entity of near apprehension. It's meant to be that way. It's the magic of hope. Now that you don't know what it is, that's what it is.

It's a circling of the mind and the heart—a gathering of energy and a royal mixing of all the feelings imaginable. And then it is a fast whirling to blend them into a beam of sunshine. That beam then becomes a showering of magic over you, one that then covers you with God's dust or all the magic that is imaginable.

Ain't that pretty? That's hope! Don't you like the hope I've brought you? And now you know that you are on a magical trip. Yes, this is a road trip of hope or another entertainment gig. It's a rolling of the wheels through potholes, pastures, meadows, lakes, streams, mountains, prairies, and the tundra. It's a road trip with no map, no destination, and no arrival or departure.

It's a magical rushing through space without a need to know why. It's floating and soaring with me and God. You have better pilots than you've ever known or could imagine. Why be afraid?

All angels know that when you give up, then you get up. Once you learn to do this, then you can get up or stand up and go on. And ironically, life is all about falling down and getting up and going on. I call this hope.

Life's also about falling face first down a mountain. Remember those scraps and bruises? They were royal ones. They required magical bandages and salve. No man-made apparatuses could have covered and protected them. They were wounds from God, and only He could heal them for you. They were wounds of hope.

The magic will see you through. I know as I now am a painter of magic and of hope and of time. I, too, missed the magic in my lifetime. I saw the trees and smelled the forests. I saw the dawn and the approaching dusk. I spread as much magic about all of this as I could. Too soon dead and too much magic.

Maybe the magic of hope and love can only be found after death. Ain't that a shame? Such magic should be grasped within each newborn baby's tiny hand. It should be a gift that arrives at the time of birth, as it's so needed and use-able. All of this is the magic of you and me together. And it's all the world needs to make it work!

It's the magic of the moment rolled up in an entity called the magic of hope. And this is what God wants in your life, in the worse way. May God and I come in to play? Human minds work a lot better if angels and celestial beings come in to stay.

THE MAGIC OF ILLNESS

(**Author's note:** All illness should be seen as a sign or a symbol that simply needs to be decoded—nothing more and nothing less. It is simply an event and one with far reaching consequences. There is never an easy answer. There is never a staged solution or not on this side. But there is always a scheduled outcome. And that is whatever is in your loved one's script.)

Being ill is like falling down a mountain, nothing more. Remember that sudden jar right after that magical moment when you floated and soared over the ground? You were free just for a second and then <u>thud</u>! That's illness.

It is a feeling of landing on something hard, possibly rough, jagged, and unfriendly. It is not a nice soft featherbed landing. It is a boom and an instant pain.

It is an awakening of the whole body to a new magic. This magic is one of wonderment. Wonder where I am? Wonder what happened? Wonder if I'll ever be the same?

It is usually followed by pain. Why can't that pain be magic, a magic of hope or a hope of a new-putting-back-togetherness? It's nothing more than a re-arranging of body parts in a new and sometimes better order. It needs to be seen as a magic of newness and betterment.

You humans have got all these labels screwed up so that no one sees the magic. It is in the hope and the tomorrow of life. This hope and magic are you and me together and is all that is needed to make everything work. Ain't it simple, just the magic of being ill and being made new again?

Sometimes the magic of illness causes death. That has its own set of magical rules, too. Just imagine the moment when all pain and sorrow cease? It's peaceful, calm, and serene. It's like none other. It's a time of being all that you can imagine. You are free and full of God's new magic for you. You are now filled with the magic of God's hope for you.

You are wild. You are free. You are everywhere. You are in love for forever. And now you are in for the ride of your life. You do know that spirits have all the fun, don't you?

Let me show you the magic of illness. Let me show you that it is an explosion of hope. And that death is the magic of hope.

THE MAGIC OF LETTING GO

(**Author's note:** Alcoholics Anonymous has a saying, "Let go and let God." Little does that organization know how far reaching this cliché truly is. Whenever you give all your power, control, and your life over to the universe (and I <u>do mean</u> give it all away), only then will you reap all the benefits of angel power. Stardom is what you are shooting for. And so are your angels who have come to help you.)

Letting go sounds simple, easy, and something that was just meant to be. You say it's different here on earth. I say that you're wrong!

Letting go means soaring with the eagles, dancing with the angels, and reaching out and playing with the moonbeams. Letting go is the freedom to be and to do everything possible. It's just the most glorious freedom to be one of God's children and to go fly away to new domains and to see new vistas.

So you don't see life this way. How come? Where did life on earth go wrong? Where did your purpose and your life change? Maybe we should look at these.

Before you returned to earth, you chose a way of life or a dream and one that you would learn from. In other words, you selected your existence.

Oh, now I know where your life went wrong. You let all sorts of human elements and earthly situations muck up your dreams, your hopes, and your lovings. And, then, too, the death of your loved one added its sadness and changes.

When a loved one dies, that person leaves you and your earth. And all just as it should be, too. But to you being left behind is not an asset, and instead it's a liability.

Haven't you ever thought long and hard about what a blessing all of this has been to both of you? That individual left you with memories and dreams and lovings. That person left you with all that you needed to survive, of course, along with God's and your angels' help. You aren't missing any pieces within yourself. You have it all.

Therefore, leaving is another gift that that person gave to you. Just how many gifts have been given to you through death? That person left you with the very best, yourself and all your attributes. So, if that's true, then how could you feel the void of anything? Leaving is actually a giving; a giving of the very best to you.

Leaving you with all the best that you can offer is just the biggest gift of all. You are the gift that you are and were meant to be. Your loved one touched your life, fulfilled one of your dreams, left you intact, and has now gone on and will await your arrival. Isn't that just the neatest gift that you could have hoped for? The gift of time on earth and the promise of another bigger and better gift in heaven.

The letting go process is God's way of telling you that your life is yours and was never ever someone else's to own and to control. This is where you went really wrong. You're all that you need. And, actually, you are all that you really and truly own. Why would you need more? Why shouldn't this be enough? Enough is what you <u>must</u> look at.

Being enough tells you that nothing can ever encompass you so totally again, not in your earthly world. You surround yourself. We surround you even more densely. And then around all of us is this entity that you call God.

Do you see the circles of light? Do you hear the magnificent sounds that are coming from all of us? Do you see that at the very center of that light is that stupendous being—you? You with all your light, your power, and your magnificent soul and way of being.

Your loved one has simply taken one step away from you and into the next circle of glorious light. He is just simply a ray of light, a moonbeam, a sun's ray away from you. You let that person step into the circle beyond your earthly realm. Therefore, you've simply let a ray of light pass through your life and out into the universe.

Letting go of one drop of sunlight is all that you've lost. All you have to do is step outside your home and catch another one. And, while you're doing that, look down at your body and your own eternal light. Now aren't you both together again in a new and more glorious light?

Letting go is simply catching a new ray of sunlight for yourself. You are that ray. You are all the light that you'll ever need. You are the dream of letting go!

You see, you're letting go of yourself—that one part of your life's dream that is finished, just as it should be. Now you can go back inside that lovely treasure chest, called you, and find the next dream that you asked for, were given, or have conjured up on your own through your God-given free will.

Letting go of that part of your dream gives you a new and unknown part of your yet undiscovered dream world—or your life script, your map of life, your heaven right here on earth. You've built a new road to yourself, to your future, and to your eventual highway to heaven. Now all you have to do is give that road a magical name. It's the road to letting go and to a brighter and better new tomorrow.

THE MAGIC OF LIFE AND YOUR LIVING

(**Author's note:** Life after a loved one's death is all about you. You now stand alone and will reap all the benefits of your being. No one is there to hold you and to teach you, except your faithful angels. They are all about living and being until your own death. They are all being your newest and bestest [sic] friends. Please write or call them, as they so like to hear messages from afar.)

Unless you take drastic steps to shorten your own life and to let all that you survey go suddenly away, you're probably going to go on living. Oh, no, you're not going to like a lot of things that you see, hear, and experience; but the fact is that your planet is what it is and all for a perfectly good reason—to learn.

Knowing this maybe I can ease you back into the living world that has eluded you since your loved one died. And there is a special magic in life and its living.

Life is another one of God's four-letter words. Notice that he's done this on purpose, for simpleness [sic] you know. Complexness is what you all have created, not God. Life is meant to be the magic of each moment, each hour, each day, each month, and each year.

Oh, how I wish you had our time frame and not one that required all these extra words to describe it. Oh, well, time, too, is one of God's simple four-letter words that has been misconstrued. There's a message in that, too; and there's always another time for you to be taught about this four-letter word.

My time here in heaven is simple, easy, and so pleasant. Remember, I did tell you that angels do have all the fun! And one day you will realize the true magnitude of what I have just said.

In contrast, your time seems heavy, long, stressful, and mostly a mess of hurryness [sic] and franticness. The life you live is exemplified by the time you keep. And you do keep it under pressure, as you're always pushing for more or using it unwisely or simply watching it by frequently looking at the nearest clock. I've always wondered if time knows how much it's watched and over loved?

Remind me to teach you how to tell time in terms of feathers. What a more precious concept this is to ease you through your days. You see, I can also make time magical and such fun.

You've had glimpses of the magic in your life. Occasionally, you've felt the lightness of a precious moment when all your real world melted away and all you felt and saw was a beautiful landscape or an evening sky or the hint of a special recognition or memory in a friend's eyes when you were talking to her.

Or, better still, the old and very wise look on a newborn baby's face and the twinkle in his eyes at the angelic wisdom that he brought into this lifetime and that he remembers so very well, but that you've nearly forgotten. All of this is magic, and all of it is true.

> The magic of life is its music
> The magic's the look of each day
> The magic's a moment of silence
> One in which your mind goes out to play
> The magic in life is its beauty
> The magic's the gleam in one's eye
> The magic's the music of laughter
> Or better still, the love you can see in the sky
> The magic is life
> And now the magic is new
> The magic's your struggle and all of your fears
> The magic's certainly all you

Now that you know where you can find your own magic for your life, you can then go back to some living, of sorts. I say of sorts, as life and its living are now truly and painfully all new.

Never before have you had to live without your special loved one. Never have you had a day to face without his presence, love, and caring—no matter how painful your life situation was with him. These things were still part of your life and your living on earth. Now this is brand new for you, as you have to count more on just you.

Just living now becomes just you in a new and more precious sense. Now you are even more your life and your living, as you have one less person on earth who loves you in that special way. But don't forget that one less person on earth means one more and bigger and greater angel in heaven to love you even more, with more intensity, at all times, and in more ways than could be on earth, and at all hours of the day or night. Ever present and ever precious means more magic for the new you.

Now your one and only choice about living is either to do it or don't do it. But remember that your newly-acquired angel and his heavenly pals are ever present to love and to protect you and to give you their advice and ever so much more support.

Ask specifically for what you need each moment of every day and night, and you will be given the magic of life. But, of course, expect even more than what you ask for, as angels like to overkill their loved ones left on earth.

You see this way they will be giving you back your living and in addition will be teaching you about other four-letter words that God so much loves to dangle in front of your pretty eyes. You see that three-letter word, God, simply stands for you, me, and him—the most important people in your every day.

See the day
Grasp my words
Find the music
Please let me be heard
The magic is you
The magic is me
The magic's all new
Just like all that you see
Ask for your angel
To ease all your pains
Watch for his answers
As you'll find even more to gain.

Please remember to write to all of us each day or more simply talk out loud and tell us how we're doing with our love and support for you. We do hate to have you bypass us with your beautiful prayers that you send only to God. We, too, need to feel, to hear, and to learn about the magic in your new life.

Angels do like celebrations, too. We love to whoop it up and to applaud loudly when your day goes well. Remember, we're jobless without you and your needs and your love.

Angels are just friends waiting for your letters and your prayers—postage free, of course, and without any long distance telephone charges. We're cheap; try us. We do come easy, and we do come free.

THE MAGIC OF LIFE'S JOURNEY

(**Author's note:** Remember all the things that you don't know. Remember all the things that you discount as just being there for you. Remember that what you're experiencing is the magic of your breathing, your energy, your joy, your sorrow, your everything. Your life is one of God's special magical events.)

Each person's life is a journey. It's a road of unknown and perhaps endless proportions, but it always ends somewhere and is very significant. Thus, there is magic in that ride.

Bet you didn't know when you opened your eyes and saw this world that your life would be such as it has been. That very first blink of your eyelids had to be more than an eye-opening experience. Imagine the beauty, the wonderment, the fear, the hope, the dismay, and every other array of conceivable thoughts and feelings. What an eye opening that was!

And as your eyes first opened into your present life here on earth, you did not know the movie-like quality that your life would take on. You say that your life isn't such. Stop and think a moment. It has to have that same quality, as you've lived it, grown from it, and experienced all that you've allowed yourself to know. If that isn't a movie, then I don't know what it is.

Within the movie of your life is the journey—the travels, the humans you've encountered, and the body and soul of what is you. Yours is like no other's journey and never will be.

How has it been? Could it have been more? Was more meant to happen? Could you have been just as happy with having less? Did you miss anything or anybody along the way? What will your life look like after it ends?

Knowing the answers to all of these questions is simply a dream away. Just ask and you will know. Within you is a special place that holds all these answers. It's known as a very special angel who can tell you if you will just ask.

One year ago you would have never imagined the events that occurred just within the last 365 days. The loss of your loved one wasn't something that you longed for. Nor was it something that you probably truly wanted.

There was no way for you to consciously know about this death or the events that would follow. Just think about that. Isn't this truly magical? Isn't this beyond your comprehension? Isn't this just a journey of magnitude proportions?

The road just traveled is exactly how your life has always been. Oh, yes, sometimes the passing year didn't contain too many lumps, bumps, curves, and barricades. On the other hand, maybe you missed them or were shielded from them as a child. Maybe they've always been there.

Just think back over each of those years of your life. Remember that life without a roadmap? Remember that life that seemed confusing and disorienting? Remember, remember, remember?

There was magic in every breath, every second, and every event. You just didn't look upon it in that fashion. See the magic in that journey? Then just think whose life are you really looking at?

Isn't that amazing that each person has such a journey? Isn't it just utterly amazing that you can only describe it as a magical event? Isn't that life amazing, particularly since it's yours and will never be repeated by anyone ever in time?

I only know what I know. And that is that your mere existence has been a total miracle and all of it magical. Look at it this way and realize that no death, no loss event, no joyous occasion occurs in and of itself. It is all part of the magic that you create by merely being alive. Alive and magic go hand in hand. And you and me together do the same.

THE MAGIC OF LONELINESS

(**Author's note:** This essay was written for someone who also loved John Denver, the singer, as much as I did. Just my knowing that this particular friend of John's was also missing him helped me to wander through each day. And wander, I did. Sudden, violent deaths always cause us survivors to intensely remember and to dwell on all kinds of imaginable memories. And all of them are good, as they are done with love.)

If I tell you that loneliness is a gift from your guardian angel, I'm just afraid that you will stop reading right now. If I tell you that it is a burden, would you do the same? What do I need to tell you about loneliness to let you know that I hear and know and have experienced what you are feeling?

How about if I tell you that loneliness is all about love? Well, your eyes did light up a bit with that statement. Now that your eyes are a bit brighter and that they show me that someone's home inside of you, let's talk about all this magic that is constantly surrounding you.

Love and death go hand in hand. And the person that is holding both the hand of death and your hand is me, the person that you so loved and now miss so terribly. You see, once your loved one is no longer on your earthly plane with you, he becomes an angel and is always there holding your hand. And, by the way, holding it out of love. Ain't that a pretty thought?

Notice that the word, loneliness, is quite similar to the word love. If you take the first four letters of loneliness (l-o-n-e) and substitute the letter "v" for the letter "n," you have the word love. Therefore, loneliness is all about loveliness. Bet you never knew that?

From my vantage point, I can now see all the love that you had for me—some so aptly expressed and some rather quiet, hidden and never totally revealed to me. I can see what I meant to you. I can see all the memories that you have about me. I can sense and know all about you and all that made you so special to me, too. Therefore, loneliness is all about loving and being even closer than you can *ever* imagine.

Yes, when I died, I did leave you alone on earth. And I am truly sorry that my death caused so much pain, grief, and endless sorrow. On the other hand, all of this has simply reinforced for me just what a magnificent person that you were to me while I was on earth.

After death, I can even see more clearly that my presence in your life was such a truly loving gift to both of us. The love went both ways. And now it's finding its way back around again in your loneliness.

Without your loneliness, you would not truly and deeply feel all the love that we shared. You know the depth of what was between us and are now to express that in a new and different way.

It may be through prayers. It may be through writing. It may be through speaking about us and our times together. It may be in song or in poetry. But whatever way it is, always know that I am listening and reading over your shoulder and sharing in your deep, vast periods of loneliness. You are never alone. Believe me, I know.

Although your times of loneliness seem to be never ending, I can tell you that they are simply a tiny, tiny grain of sand, a miniscule drop of fresh water in the springtime, or just a special gleam in a ray of sunlight. No matter what you believe, your time is short, your life is even shorter—according to my heavenly timetable.

You see, loneliness is the time that you're spending in the loveliness of our relationship. Being lonely is all about loving. So when you feel that you're way too lonely for way too much of the time, then just look upon it as tons of time that we are still loving each other and being in the other one's life.

And as you wallow in loneliness — if that is what you need to do — simply please — ask me to come be with you. I will sit by your side and hold your hand and enfold you in my arms. And let's wallow in our love for each other.

Wallowing in love is really a fun and magical activity. Can I come join you? All you have to do is say my name out loud, and I will come and join your time of remembering and loving me.

The magic of loneliness lies in the love that we always shared. And I do mean that it is magic. Just think about which folks you feel lonely about after their deaths. If there are no lonely feelings after such an event, then the magic of the love between you was also missing in that relationship.

Love and magic and loneliness are a happy threesome. The magic of love is the time that you and I shared on earth, and now the magic that I am sharing with you is through loneliness. Not only are you now talking to an angel and loving me again, but you are also talking to yourself. Talk to me, and I'll help you to find the love for yourself again.

We are both in this magic called loneliness that so often surrounds you. It takes two, you know. Wanna talk about it and about love and about magic?

And you know, I have all the right answers. Wanna bet? Bet I can top you with my advanced knowledge about magic. *I'll bet you anything.*

THE MAGIC OF LOSING IT

(**Author's note:** I truly can't remember a time in my life when I didn't feel like I was losing it. Never fitting in to the life on this planet has always been a struggle. And after the death of my loved one, I found that I frequently went to hide in being lost and alone and definitely on some foreign highway. It will always be a daily struggle, but it's much easier knowing that I am not too unusual and now I am definitely not alone.)

Losing it doesn't have to be a bad thing. It can simply mean that you're growing and knowing. The letting go of all that is past is a time of great excitement. Once this is done, then the knowing can take place, the new knowing that one needs to go on with life.

Losing it can also mean that God is giving you new gifts to treasure and to love. And then there are the gifts you are receiving right now from me, too. They're the gift of being with me in a different place and time.

The beauty of this is in the process. If you're feeling less than normal right now, don't despair, as I am only a breath away, a smile away, a kiss away. I'm always here, just look and ask and hear.

At this point in the process, you're tending to shut down. This can simply mean that I am coming in much stronger and that God is also blessing you with the gift of hope. Hope, remember, is that paralyzing feeling that you've had so many times before.

Hope is also a veil of anticipation. It's not always a pleasant feeling for you. Sometimes it is that utterly paralyzing feeling of being incapable of functioning. That's hope, and right now you are filled to over flowing with it. And it is something that you or no one else can see or touch.

Just take all of this as a gift from me and God and not something to worry about. This hope is also filled with a great peace of mind. Look for it, and it will become even more obvious to you. The magic of hope is having me around to prop you up when you want to collapse and die, too.

Losing it simply means that you have totally given yourself to me and to mine. It simply means that all is well from where we view the world. And simply means that for once you have given everything away and are totally free and open to our gifts for you.

Losing it also means that you no longer have to hang on to the reality that you once knew. Now your life is one of going for it all, and no one is standing there giving you another opinion of who and what you are about. And you now have our blessings and our love to take the place of what you have lost.

Therefore, the magic of losing it means that no longer do you have to be a person that is in pain. You no longer have to look at the world and how it affects your loved one. Now the knowings that you have will circle around you and lighten up your life. And the life that you now have is one that will never be lost, never be condemned, and never be seen as something that you need to atone for.

The night is now yours. The day is all for you. And all this means is that I am your guiding light. And with you and me together, you can never lose it again. Why? Because all that I have is now yours, for now and for all time. The magic of losing it is gaining a friend from afar. And that's both you and me together—you know, in that all too distant star.

THE MAGIC OF LOSS

(**Author's note:** Loss is another four-lettered word. It describes a situation which you think you are entitled to avoid. Being a human being, I suggest that you think again. Every second of every day is some type of loss—big, small, noticed, or unknown and unfelt. You can't avoid it, so you'd better realize that it's magic in disguise.)

Loss is such a horrendous thing for the survivors. At no time does it make any sense. At no time do the feelings ever totally disappear. At no time does the beauty of the experience really manifest itself as it could. Or does it?

Just remembering your beloved friend or loved one and all that he meant to you is such a treasure. All those good times; all those iffy times. All those other times in between. What do you suppose that he remembers? Do you ever stop to think of that?

Even the angels have thoughts and memories of their time on earth and all those special beings that meant so much to them. To know and to remember those folks is a treasure that can never be replaced, nowhere in time. To have a rich history of loved ones who mourn and miss you is such a blessed gift. The gift is truly one that is a blessing for both the survivor and the deceased.

What is a loss? It is simply a moment in time, a second in the universe. On earth it could be a lifetime of grieving and sadness. In heaven it's a tiny fraction of an entire life. In both places, it is a drop of love that was sent out into the world and will be returned many times to the owner and to that special person who remembers and deeply cares.

Is it really a loss? Why, no! How could a drop of love ever be a loss? The love that was shared and freely given will only manifest itself and grow and grow and grow. Love planted always blooms again.

You perhaps feel that you have nothing to hang on to. What does hanging on mean? Does it mean in the sense of a material possession? Does it mean something like a human body to enfold in your arms and a shoulder to cry on? Does it mean a lifetime dream and a hope for your future? Does it mean not having that special person to talk to here on earth?

Why do you need something to hang on to? Your angel friend is doing all of the holding now. And by that, I mean that he's hanging on to you. You're never far away from him. He's right there beside you all the time.

He's watching and waiting for you to stumble and fall. He's the first person to reach out to you and to help you once again to your feet. He not only hears your pleas for comfort, for love, and for strength; but he even tries to anticipate them. But angels cannot *read* your mind. You must ask and tell him what you really need from him or for him to do for you.

How do you know he's right there beside you? Well, just ask some flippant question out loud and see what answer you get from the angel world. When it's some answer that you could never think up—even if you stayed up all day and all night for the rest of your life—then you know that you're receiving an answer from your loved one who is now your special angel. If you get a really, off-the-wall, smart-mouthed response, you'll know for sure just who is whispering in your ear and possibly teasing you and egging you on.

Angels will do anything to get your attention. And then they will care for you and love you until you recover from your heavenly shock of truly being heard. Messages sent mean messages are always received in time and with unbounded love.

Remember that angels communicate with you by using words that you understand. And some even swear and get angry if you don't listen to them. Be prepared for every kind of response imaginable. And by all means please listen to your own requests, questions, and longings.

Ask, listen closely and intensely, and demand that your deceased loved one talk to you in plain, simple, easy-to-understand English. I'm just sure that you're going to try this and find that you'll get some of the weirdest answers imaginable.

When you ask for this person to come and to be your guardian angel, you know that he'll do just that. How can he turn down requests that are so gut-wrenching and from a person that loved him so dearly?

Did he ever turn away from you before? Did he ever refuse to be your friend here on earth? Did he ever seem to be far away then? Well, all of these things were true while he was on earth and are even more true today. He's no farther away than your simple request to ask him to come and to be with you.

The magic of loss is simply an angelic moment. And that moment is within your grasp. It's just a breath away, a dream away, or an ASK away. The magic, you see, lies within yourself. Now you can make anything magical happen. The power is yours. And then the gift will be both yours and his.

THE MAGIC OF MAKIN'
BELIEVERS

(**Author's note:** A believer can look exactly like you and me. And yet that being has a very special angelic quality. It's almost like a special eyesight, a special gait to his walk, a special smile like he knows. He may look very human like, but he has a heart like no other, a soul that you truly believe in, and the time of day to waste endlessly on you. He'll make you into a believer, as right now it is more than I can do.)

The makin' of believers concerning all this magic surrounding death is not your task to undertake. Makin' believers is my department and God's. You have no control over this and should never concern yourself about this. We're much more adept in this department and hold all the cards. Well, actually, we not only hold them, we even made them.

Believers! I wonder what that word means. I wonder if it means making knowers [sic]. I wonder if it means making tellers. I wonder if it means just enlightening folks. I wonder if it means that knowing, believing, and being enlightened go hand in hand.

I wonder if even I know the true meaning of this word. My stab at a definition is using all my love to make folks happy. Now, that's a believer in my book.

Makin' believers has to be the key to all this love that I am here to impart and to share and to spread around the universe. My words should be able to tell you that this is a happy task for me and one that I am so well qualified to do.

Spreading love and peace and understanding was my mission in my earthly life. And I did it so well. I conveyed everything that I knew in the most simplistic and direct way. I gave each of you many love letters.

I gave each of you the very best of me. I talked to each of you with your own personal message. I showed you that I cared about you. I sang to you of times and places and love.

My love was endless and always flowing. I spread as much love as I could around your planet. The believers heard and shared and conveyed their own personal love to even more beings.

The process never changed. The message always stayed the same. And the love was given and shared endlessly and unconditionally. Love was the master that I served.

Now the believers are hearing me from a distance, from a faraway place and yet one that is even closer to each of you. My love for the planet and the beings is still my message.

I am now everywhere that I want to be. I am up close and personal with each and every one of you. I am just a breath away, a word within your every reach, a touch of such gentle kindness—a love that I've come to share again.

If you'll just ask, I promise to come to you. I serve all of you, as you are now my eternal masters. I can very quickly tune into each of your varied needs and wants and longings. I can hear you so clearly and simplistically when you ask for me to come and to share your life and your traumas.

I know intuitively all of your feelings, fears, and longings. I have no trouble comprehending and decoding any of your messages. There is no chance that I will make an error in my communication from you and to you.

All is complete. All is perfect. All is just as it should be. I am just a breath away from you right now. Can't you feel me ever near your physical being?

Once you hear me in a new form and listen to my profound messages, you will never again doubt my presence and my love. All that I know and am and will ever be are readily accessible to you. Right now, right here, right in this very moment.

Ask, listen, and come be with me and mine. I am the person that will make you the believer, as you now have no other choice in this matter. You are now compelled to reach out and touch me and know that what I am saying is true.

I am the believer. I am the person who loves you so much and cares for your every need. I am the one that you reach for during your empty hours and nights. I am the one that is there to cradle and to croon to you. I am the holder. I am your knight in shining armor. I am all that you long for. I am the believer.

I will share my words with you and pray like mad that you listen and let my messages soak into your heart and mind and that you will open up your ears to be able to hear me. I am in your every sigh. I am a part of all your tears. I am playfully in your giggles and moments of merriment. I am in all your fears. I am the biggest part of each longing. I am that dream that awaits you in your nights.

I am the sunshine of your mornings. I am that bird outside your window. I am that breeze that wafts across your cheek. I am the chill in the air of those glorious winter nights and within each snowflake that always lands in just that special spot on earth. The rain contains my cleansing qualities and brings you that delicious smell of newness and earthly delights.

Never ask where I am, as you already know. Me, the believer, is all around you and am always helping you through your days. I am you. You are me. We are one. There are no doubts. There are no fears.

There is only love within this old believer. And that very special love is all that I hold in my heart for you. Believers are lovers! And I'm the master of the lovers.

Know my love and believe in it. Then all will be simple for you. All will come true. All will be magical. You will then know the magic of makin' believers, and it's *so much fun to do*!

THE MAGIC OF NOTHINGNESS

(**Author's note:** After my loved one's death, I sat for hours and hours and wrote. Obviously I did this as there was nothing else to do that made sense. My world was upside down, my feelings were shattered, and more than half of my life had disappeared. No one saw, few came, and rarely did anyone want to understand me. Nothingness and my writings began to take on a whole new meaning—lots of nothingness that was put into many, many words.)

When you have nothing in your life, that is when you own and possess everything. When you see nothingness in your day, that is when we as angels are most at play.

When nothingness seems safe and warm, that is when you truly hear that infamous, far-off horn. And when nothingness is what you crave, you have come to the right store to shop for it, your ever-loving Angel Store of Nothingness.

Can't you see the marquee out front? Can't you imagine that golden writing on it? Can't you see the individual angels who are hanging out at the store today? How can you pass by when so many of your own angels are beckoning you to come in? How can you give up a chance to come play with us?

Cause, guess what? We're going to play in your mind today whether you choose to join us or not. Best get on board and ride away into the land of nothingness with us. It's free. Come and be just like me.

Today was another one of your far out days. It was one of those times when all you could do was make lists of things. In this case, it was a list of how nothingness is affecting you. And death always does this to you. You see in your earthly sense that death takes away from you. Not so! Never has been and never will be.

If death takes something away from you, then by now (or at your somewhat advanced age), you really should have nothing left to cope with. Ain't it strange that you are taught in your earthly world that older folks know how to cope better than younger ones do? If they have had so many losses in life, it seems to me that they should not be coping at all. Strange, is it not? That coping and nothingness have nothing to do with each other.

Coping is your earthly word for making sense out of something that you long to understand. And that something is death. And let me tell you that if you ever learn to interpret it in earthly terms, I plan to come and blow all of your meanings away. You see, coping and death should never ever be used in the same sentence.

Coping is about your world. And death is about my world and where I now live. Coping is a word defined in your dictionaries, but death is a word that only God and us can define for you. Magic, you know.

Nothingness is all about magic. You should have guessed this by now. Nothingness is simply floating along and observing and loving what you don't have.

But let's face it, some days should be about loving yourself and the feelings that God has given you. But for right now, all you seem to be able to do is love the nothingness of your physical world. And at the same time, you are longing for the reoccupation of the vastness of your spiritual realm. Or, in other words, where I now live.

Here are your interpretations of the word, nothingness, from one of your infamous lists that you compiled so thoroughly on your off days after your loved one's death:

Nothingness is starring out the window
Nothingness is having no time and no space
Nothingness is watching the leaves blow
Nothingness is being nowhere
Nothingness is hoping for nothing
Nothingness is an absence of fear
Nothingness is knowing the truth
Nothingness is having the answer
Nothingness is wallowing in the moment
Nothingness is not waking up
Nothingness is not feeling again
Nothingness is time pulling tricks on you
Nothingness is going nowhere in your mind
Nothingness is returning from nowhere
Nothingness is sitting and sitting and sitting
Nothingness is everything
Nothingness is you
Nothingness is your lover
Nothingness is your family
Nothingness is your loved one and not having him on earth
Nothingness is empty tears
Nothingness is simply you and me together

So what do you want to argue about in all this magic of nothingness? Seems simple and straightforward to me. Ask for nothingness. Recognize when it comes. Shop for it deliberately. And then ask in all innocence, "Where is this space called you and me?"

In the magic that you are now experiencing is that which you, too, will know as you get closer to your own death. What is this? It's the magic of the universe. It's the magic of love. It's the magic of holding on to nothing and yet experiencing the thrill of having and possessing everything.

Now try to tell me that your loved one is afraid of his future, his loves, and his new space in the universe. If he isn't and he already knows the truth, then why are you fighting the magic of the nothingness that he already is beginning to see?

In the nothingness and its magical powers, you will see yourself. You will see me. And, best yet, you will again see your loved one. His death means that you are simply gaining a new angel. And this is one that will truly always be with you. Ask and ye shall receive all the magic of the nothingness of God's universe, you know, that simple fact of just you and me.

How long is it going to take for you to learn to love the magic of your nothingness? Oh, well, I have nothing to do but sit and wait right here beside you. Want to play cards while we wait? How about bridge? Want to write a song? How about a song about the magic of the nothingness?

How about talking to me, your favorite angel, about how you aren't too sure that I am really sitting here beside you? Want an answer that you can hear? Bet that would surely convince you about the magic of your nothingness. Want to try? It's really magic, you know.

THE MAGIC OF PEACE

(**Author's note:** I can easily make peace with death, both my own and others, too. It's planet earth that I have trouble with. There are so many definitions of peace, and so many meanings that I don't understand. I know what peace means in heaven, but here where I live I don't believe that I have found it. And I wonder if I ever will.)

Peace and death go hand in hand, although few people look at these events in this manner. And <u>manner</u> is the key word here. The manner in which you go into the dying process determines where, when, and how you find your peace.

Oh, sure, it's really easy to say that a loved one who has suffered immensely is now dead and at peace. And most folks can even sort of justify this in their minds and souls. <u>Almost</u> is the key word here.

And death is the best almost word that I can think of. Very, very few people totally and willingly accept death as an event that is meant to be and all in good time and in an appropriate fashion. Maybe there are in reality no folks who totally accept death.

Funny, isn't it, that one event which can bring you the most peace in your life has an almost and maybe-not-for-sure quality to it. Must be meant to be this way, as God is certainly the only individual in your life who runs on for-sure-time and always on a meant-to-be schedule.

Interesting and even more interesting is that death is so definite, so final, and so real. And now it is even more interesting that it is the biggest almost event in your modern life. But in your society, it is almost *not an event*.

Once your loved one's death has happened, you ring up all your friends and acquaintances and hurry to set up a funeral or a memorial service. Get it over with and go on seems to be the philosophy of your modern world. Modern for whom?

When you talk in terms of what's modern today and what's old-fashioned, then you begin to talk at both ends of the spectrum. Just think about what was old-fashioned in your youth and just what happened to work. Well, now think about today. What is now out of date for today's world but is working for you?

Working is the key, and labeling the old and the new is a waste of man's words. Note that I said man's words, as God never wastes his time on labeling anything. Star power, you know. And then there's heavenly pride. Goes hand in hand to make a special individual, just like you and me.

Where is there peace to find in a death situation? Well, first, start looking for the miracles that are happening all around you. These may be interesting phrases that folks use, maybe unusual terms and unknown words. There may be the dreams where deceased love ones come to pay a visit and to give love and hope and encouragement. Any angel will do. And all of them do the best job always.

These happenstances will tell you for sure that magic is occurring and that you'd better fess up to just how extraordinary this occasion is going to be. You see, if the magic is seen in the dying process then the peace and all its magic are not far behind.

But first you have to tune into the magic of death, not only your loved one's experiences but your own, too. You know all those emotions that you call traumatic and stressful and full of situations where loved ones want to pick a fight? Well, these are just the beginning of the peace that is to come. But first comes the magic that you don't see.

Next, be careful that you don't miss the angel dust and the glow from your loved one. And be sure to ask your own angels to decipher the magic that is being measured out for you. And, oh, yes, it does come in measurements. Sort of like cups of love and support and caring. Sort of like magic in its best form, all and only for you.

And when the dust has settled
And you've got time to look around
Just notice where the angel dust
Has been piled and can be found

Look in all the cracks and crevases
Look and see where you glow
Take the time to see the difference
And just and for always let us know

We can pile on heaps of loving
Glowing greatness to behold
But if it goes away unnoticed
Then God and all will feel so cold

Failure's not a virtue
Not in my heavenly realm
As all that's seen around me
Is more than heaps to be found

The peace from your loved one's death is truly magical and all around you. This peace may come in different colors and in different shades or hues. Redness may denote pain to some, while to others it's just a magnificent glow and a promise of motivation and the goodness to come.

Don't listen to the experts who have designated colors for certain emotions. Now you're on God's color palette and earthly meaning holds no truths. And within this palette, you will be given your own peace, your own colors, and your own sense of death. Because it is only when you see death as you want it to be do you find the peace you need.

Peace and death and love and magic . . . what more can I say to tell you about the magic of peace. Well, I guess that I could throw in joy and happiness, too. And then there is always hope and anticipation and freedom and wings. *And, NO, I am NOT talking about feathers.*

Best choose all the magical words that you can find. These denote peace for you. And I'll throw in all the magic that I can deliver. There you go again, it's simply the magic of you and me together.

Lastly, the magic of knowing is that all is well and just as it was meant to be, full of magic and of me. If I hadn't told you this, you may never have equated death and peace. And if I hadn't revealed this to you, then you may never have discovered it until the moment of your own death.

But peace and magic are too special to keep hidden. And nothing can stay hidden for forever, not even God and magic and death and all its peace. And, oh, if I haven't already told you, peace is also excitement.

And if you can't conjure up some excitement about this magical peace that I live with each day, well, then I'd better go back to angel school where peace is our number one class. And, of course, it's only taught from the magical viewpoint. Bigger magic means bigger peace—one for all and all for all time.

THE MAGIC OF PRAYING

(**Author's note:** After my loved one died, my sister blatantly told me that prayers had to follow a precise format. Made me mad as hell! How dare anyone tell a grieving person how to pray? How dare anyone impose their earthly wisdom on anyone else, particularly one like me who had a live-in angel who described all that I was experiencing in such a healthy way? This is when I came up with my favorite cliché: "You have a right to your opinion, and you have a right to keep it to yourself.")

Well, my lovely friend, your form of praying is not one to be found in church books. Let's just sort of say that it works, in your own unique and uncanny way. No, I'm not going to spill your endearing names for me. Best I keep my bread buttered just so. And when it comes to saying prayers, believe me, anything and everything does work.

Whoever laid down do's and don'ts for saying prayers must be coming from a different place than you and me. I guess we're maverick angels, one here in heaven and one still on earth.

Let me tell the world about your form of praying. I know that there are more wonderful folks like you who have to be God's children, just as he made them. You cannot and must not alter your special way of being just to conform to a heavenly format, in the hope of being better heard by God and your angels.

This is not necessary, and actually I think I'd readily doze off if you didn't throw in your endearing terms to wake me up. Not one day has ever been dull, since I've come to live with you and to constantly deliver your gift for the rest of your life, a job of love.

Just when I know that you have learned so very much about my magic, you throw in one of your favorite slang words that so aptly describes your concept of me. And you use such blatant earthly terms. You don't think that that doesn't wake up me and God and your fleet of angels? Think again, darlin'.

You rattle our cages, our minds, and our heavenly dimensions. No prayer of yours is ever complacent, anticipated in its entirety, or ignored. Doesn't that ease your mind about those old-fashioned things that you were taught; for example, God's gonna get you for this or that? This should relieve all your fears, doubts, and free you to just be yourself.

My messages about prayers are always the same. Be yourself! Be real! Be direct! Be demanding! Be specific!

Sweetheart, none of us can read your mind. But we all certainly sit up and take notice when you chew us out or praise us to the hilt or tearfully behoove us to jump to and to come to your aid right now.

Thankfully, there is no book up here that says that prayers have to be a certain way. There's no manual for poor humans who are going on and growing and becoming more knowing. All words and feelings are acceptable. Please remember that we have ears of steel.

Our only job is to catch each of your prayers that you utter, and best you do this out loud. And the louder the better! We do like heavenly noises that are sent our way. The more, the better too.

What do we do with each of your prayers after it is received? Well, of course, we first check your life's script. If your request can be delivered today, we do it. If the timing is off, then we make a note and do it for you when the time's right.

If your plea is not one that can be delivered in your requested format, then we alter it to accommodate your life's plan. If we can deliver even more gifts to you today, then we happily and quickly do this.

If your request is not one that is part of your earthly life, we send you a replacement offer of love. Always and for forever, a gift does come your way to answer your prayer. Now this gift may be more symbolic than actual. Therefore, you must look, listen, and watch for your answer to your prayer. But the magic in a prayer is always yours, and it is the magic of you and us and togetherness.

Please exercise your free gift of prayer as often as possible. We love hearing from you. We love your magical messages. We *so much* love to be included in your day. We *so much* want to be one with you. Please share the magic with us and let us give you all our love and magic, too.

THE MAGIC OF
PROCRASTINATION

(**Author's note:** Earthly tasks seem so time consuming and so many times not worth it. Therefore, I have learned to put off until tomorrow all of today, the next day, the next week, the next month, and even next year. Has it served me well? Must have, because I am still alive and still productive, sort of. And death gave me a huge excuse to wallow and wait and wonder. And through this process Wise Eagle came to live with me.)

What does procrastination have to do with death? Lots! Cause death does lots of goofy things to your mind. And one of these is causing you to lose interest in the real world in which you are merely and barely existing.

Procrastination is a feeling of always being overwhelmed, of feeling as though you're merely treading water, and of caring less if you do your mundane chores. Caring less is not quite it. It's more like having already drowned and not even having the strength to check out this possibility.

This is more like a feeling of trying to put off everything until after you, too, die. It's a feeling of saying to yourself, "Death would do the trick—my death, that is. At that point there would be no more of this feeling. Yes!"

This inactivity in your mind prevents you from doing the things that you really need to do. But, in addition, it provides you with a dance; a dance without music, but one of avoidance and escape. Within this dance is the music of the mind; the song being, "Let Me Out Of Here!" It goes something like this:

The world's a place of despair
What's the use of living there?
There's time to waste
And time to savor
This sure ain't one
That's in my favor.

Chorus:

Let me avoid
Let me deny
Let me just get by
Let me out of here

What does this say about you? It says that you're extremely troubled and definitely are in need of divine intervention. To recapture the normal essence of yourself, you need the help of God and your guardian angels.

What do you ask for? You merely demand of them: "Help me right now. Talk to me in plain English and complete sentences. Come and tell me how to reactivate my mind."

You say that this sounds too simple. Not! All you have to do is try it once and see that it works. Then you, too, will always be a believer in the spirit world and all that it can do for you.

The solution is simple. The process is painless. The cost is free. What more can you ask for? Will it bring results? You bet!

The procrastination of the mind is God's way of saying: *Stop! Look! Listen!* <u>Stop</u> wallowing in grief. <u>Look</u> at the possibilities and ask for help. <u>Listen</u> to your guardian angels and follow their advice.

The world of hope and peace and love is always surrounding you. And all you need to do is ask for help. God never withholds it, never denies you your total share, and always lovingly answers your pleas. In addition, he acquaints you with new friends from afar and encourages you to always talk to them and to love them as much as they love you. Peace!

Life's simple
Life's free
Life's a gift of you
And comes from God and me.

THE MAGIC OF REALITY

(**Author's note:** Since death is final on this planet, reality often jumped up and bit me before I could assess its pluses and minuses. Every day was far too real and far too up close and personal. Teaching about death and dying was one thing. Experiencing it for myself made me realize that there were no rules that I had to follow except paying estate taxes and following the laws. Therefore, my reality became one of writing my own rules for grieving and dealing with friends and relatives.)

Reality, you say? What more is there to learn about it? Death's eminent or has already occurred. How much more real can all this get? Maybe it doesn't need to get real, but maybe it just needs to be examined in a little different light. In fact, maybe just putting some light on reality will soften its effects and make you less edgy.

Reality is simple God's way of saying, "Welcome to my world; welcome to my day." The beauty of God's world is that he cares deeply about you and your plight. He wants nothing more for you than peace and happiness. Unfortunately, to attain these you must also deal with the facts of life.

When God gave your loved one life, he also gave that person the hope and the beauty of death and that is being with God for eternity. Now, that gift and its magic meant that all other gifts must also be looked upon as magical. What other way is there to look at it?

One of such gifts is reality. Isn't that simple? I'm sure that you don't think so at this point in time. Your loved one is leaving you to function alone and on your own. That person is going to leave a void in your life. Now your life will be changed for forever. And here I am trying to tell you that there's some magic in the reality of death.

Where's the rhyme, and where's the reason? The rhyme is that peace and happiness will follow this event in your life. At no time did God ever withhold this from his loved ones. The reason in all this is that to attain such satisfaction, you will need to pass through an area that you label reality. I label it the Valley of Hope.

Here again all sorts of hope will jump up and join you in the journey through this valley. There's the hope that you will live through this time. There's the hope that the sun will come up tomorrow. There's the hope that all will be well with your life once again. There's hope that you will arrive at a new destination and be a new and happier you.

Where will you get all this hope? From God, of course. He's going to see that you have every bit of hope for all things right and good. Oh sure, he may let you play with your mind a bit. He'll allow you to wallow in your reality. Then out of nowhere, BOOM, there will appear a ray of hope. Never will he let you be so downtrodden that you cannot find some hope to cling to and to help you through the storm of reality.

Reality has lots of forms. It may be unpleasant feelings that you're experiencing as the result of death. It may be the panic that you feel at having to be fully in charge of yourself, your finances, and other legal matters. It may the knowledge that there are additional burdens as the result of this death. Not to worry; the reality is that a new and different realness is going to occur—not only with you personally but also with your relationship with your loved one.

The Valley of Hope is really a warm and gentle place with a few sharp rocks sticking out of the sidewalls that may give you a few scratches and bruises. But those places don't have to be scaled alone. And you may take someone with you to assist you through the areas where you have less expertise.

If it's simply for moral support, your guardian angel is always a big help. Other times you can ask the professionals in your life to accompany you or to show you how to deal with various situations. Most importantly, if you're a parent be sure to ask your children for their input.

Remember that those younger folks in your life often see the world a little more clearly; and most importantly, intellectually they're far brighter than you are. It's so important to allow children to be a part of the reality of death and its consequences.

See, you don't have to share the burdens alone. Help is simply standing close by and waiting for you to ask for assistance.

So what's the light that I'm shedding on reality? Reality is simply the knowledge that you need to make the changes in your life. Knowledge is always a light; not always soft and dim, but sometimes it's glaring and harsh.

Can the intensity of this light be changed? Sure! These lights have dimmer switches, you know those round things on your wall plate where you can turn the light up or down and make it just to your liking. Perhaps it's as simple as, how many folks is it going to take to turn that switch up or down so that just the right amount of knowledge comes into your life to make you more comfortable? Sounds like a bad joke? Could be!

On the other hand, think on this. The reality and its magic are simply assessing how much realness you can handle today. Once this is known, then find the folks to help you turn that dimmer switch up or down or in between.

So, in the beginning it takes a few more people to keep your light of reality in its proper perspective. This won't always stay this way. Soon you'll be able to once again deal with the magic of reality. It may take a little time, but during this process the assistance that you receive will help you to see the magic in the process and its gift to you.

THE MAGIC OF REMEMBERING

(**Author's note:** You must be very careful in your remembering. Some days are better to look back. And some days forward is all there is for you. Do remember that your loved one's imprint is on everything that was associated with him. His energy is in that item, and his feelings about you still surround you. Remember to remember only if it is a pleasant activity for you.)

Remembering your loved one is such a treasured event. It's one that is unique and truly and absolutely one-of-a-kind. It should be done when you want to do it and should never be forced upon you. Now, of course, this is utopia. And God knows that you live in a terribly unperfect [sic] world.

Unfortunately, other folks do not know how unsolicited remembering affects you. And affect you they do! Even the most benign remark, such as, "How are you today?" may trigger more memories than you want to think about at that time.

Of course, that other person has no idea that such a remark takes you back in time or forward in time. It may regress you to a period when your feelings were so raw and so close to the surface. Or it may project you into the future when you hope that you never ever have another feeling about anything.

Bless those folks' hearts and their gifts of caring. They mean so well, and you must look upon their remarks as blessed gifts. They cared enough to acknowledge your presence on earth today. Please do thank them for doing this.

At other times the question, "How are you?" will simply go right over your head. Then you'll reply, "Fine," and go on your merry way. And this is what most folks assume that they will hear from you, but you just never know how you are going to react.

Thus, remembering is like leafing through the scrapbook in your mind. As thoughts, symbols, and feelings emerge, you see and remember so well what your loved one was like and all the good times and the bad ones, too. Remembering can also be described as replaying that video in your head for that portion of your life that is no more.

If you are having a good day, then those replays will be amusing, loving, and so dear to you. You will relish those pretty pictures, those happy times, and all the fun that you had. Those memories are the ones that you keep close to your heart and that sustain you through your nights.

On the other hand, if you are forced to remember something that causes you to feel sad, then you're likely to have every type of reaction imaginable. Just thoughts of him, just beautiful pictures of him, or anything will push you over the edge and make you wonder if you're longing to be with him will ever end.

Such remembering can make you feel as though you are suffocating. Somehow, the breath is virtually sucked out of you; and it might be so difficult to breathe. Or the scab on that hole in your heart that never totally heals may begin to move again and to come unglued around the edges. What a painful feeling that is!

You perhaps may feel as though someone has unzipped that human suit that you wear and has literally turned your physical body inside out. Now all your feelings and innards are exposed to the elements, and there is literally no place for you to hide. *Now, what an open wound you are!* Your entire body inside and out is just a gigantic open, walking sore—bleeding, weeping, so irritated.

You might also feel as though you have suddenly lost all your muscle tone, your bone structure, everything inside your body. You may feel so weak that it takes considerable effort to just move your arms, your head, and your legs. This is certainly the weakness that surpasses all earthly understanding.

The magic of remembering is that you control all the buttons on the video recorder in your mind. There's a button for you. There's a button for me. There's a button for God. Watch which one you select.

If you push your button, your mind can go backward, forward, and stay in the present and all at the same time. This is the button of profound confusion. Your button never works well by itself. You just think that it should, it does, and that it just might— if you pushed it one more time. Not!

If you push the button with your guardian angel's name on it, you will get a beautiful reply that is not only picturesque but is also carefully guided and annotated. I'll explain and guide and love and hold you as your memories unfold within your heart and your mind. This one's a trip through time in a lovely bubble of white light or pink light, or whatever your favorite color is.

God's button on that machine is the one that makes all things perfectly clear and always in the right perspective. And, the best part is that this button only operates in conjunction with yours and mine. Ain't that a nice threesome? Now, how many buttons do you need to push and all at the same time?

And, so, the magic of remembering is not something that you ever do alone as you perceive it to be. When you remember, you're really calling up all your angels and God, and asking all of us to join in your memories, in your loves, and in your sorrows.

The magic is then revealed in the warmth that surrounds you, in the tears that stream down your face, and in the inner glow that is now radiating outward and surrounding you. You see the magic of remembering is actually the beauty and the solace that emerges from the inside of your body and your mind. There's beauty in the magic of remembering.

It's the magic of you and me together, in the good times and in the bad. It's the magic of each moment that you have lived. It's the magic in what you don't know, and in what I can bring to you and teach you. It's the magic of this infamous threesome acting as one. Please push all the right buttons.

THE MAGIC OF SAYING GOODBYE

(**Author's note:** Saying good-bye is not for everyone. I have my own stages of grieving and probably rewrite them for each individual death that I experience. I try to say my psychological goodbyes in a timely fashion. But sometimes the scab on my broken heart comes off and my tears are as painful and as prolific as the day that my loved one died. Sometimes final good-byes are just not doable. Don't do what you cannot do.)

Saying good-bye to a loved one is truly magical. In reality, what you are doing is saying good-bye to that person and then saying hello to yourself. Because, in fact, you are not the same person who said hello to that individual many, many days or years ago. And it is best to tell your loved one in person and before he dies all your thoughts, feelings, and longings.

Are you really saying good-bye? No, you're saying hello to a new you and to a new spirit in your life. You're just simply changing your status with yourself and with your loved one. Simple? Sure.

You might label this process as scary. Not! That scariness is simply excitement, the excitement of all the newness that it will produce for both of you. Excitement is in the magic of the process and the results. Try it. You're really going to like it.

What do you do first? You cue in on all your thoughts and feelings surrounding your loved one and your life together. Write down everything that you're thinking about, and I do mean everything. Best not let any topic go unnoticed.

Remember you are now beginning to operate on God's time and in his world, and this is much different than yours here on earth. It's magical and loving and true. It's the perfect world that you long for.

What should you ask and/or say? Everything! Best start with the "I loved you when . . . ." statements. My favorite thing to do is to always tell the other person about the gift he was and is to me and always will be.

Can't you just see that look of joy and honor and praise on the other person's face when you sit down and give him this gift? It will be one of wonderment, utter beauty, and such happiness. This is truly unresistible [sic]!

From here you tell each other your favorite moments with one another. This includes such things as:

I will always remember . . . .
Gee, I wish we could have done . . . .
I will always be grateful for . . . .
I am always going to miss you . . . .
I will always love you for . . . .
Holidays will never be the same, because . . . .

Of course, you must not forget those other moments and feelings when you were upset with each other and had disagreements. To talk about these things is going to take real courage on both of your parts.

This is the time when you will need to take a great big breath, look deep inside yourself, and ask for God and your guardian angels to come and help you. You need all the help that you can get, as you are going to say the least desirable things about your relationship with this person.

And, oh, yes, best call up your loved one's guardian angels, too. And go ahead and throw God into the mix for heavenly luck you know.

For example:

I was really upset when . . . .
I would like to forgive you for . . .; can you help me?
I want to forget about . . . .
I was hurt when . . . .
I want us to forgive each other for . . . .

Learning about your loved one's past is also so important. Remember that now is the time to tap into that library of information that only that person knows. The books of the past are written in the human mind. And some things that you might like to know are:

Tell me about your parents and your other relatives.
Tell me what they taught you.
Tell me about you as a child; your toys, your dreams, your
    hopes, your fears.
Tell me about the good times.
Tell me about the bad times.
Tell me about your concept of heaven, or where you're
    going after death.
Tell me everything that you remember about your life on
    earth.

The final and most important thing to tell your loved one is that you are capable of going on without him. Each person needs to know that his death will not destroy another's life.

In addition, you will need to tell the dying person that you are ready for him to die. Some folks need permission to let go of life. Often times the dying person will hold on for one specific individual—perhaps a child that he is worried about; perhaps a friend who needs him to stay alive; perhaps a spouse who is just not yet ready to let go of his human form.

Another bit of information that you might like to have in your library for the future are the plans that your loved one has for you. "What do you want me to do in the future? Should I remarry? What are your hopes and dreams for me? How will I know that you are talking to me from heaven? Will you reappear for me so that I can see and touch you again? How will I know that you are still loving me and are really here helping me? Please tell me what to look for."

Are these good-byes just to be said to a dying person? No, no, no! These are things that you need to say and to discuss with everyone that you truly love and care about. And you need to do this every single day of your life. This is God's glue that makes the world a better place.

You must do these things every day. God knows that your loved ones need to hear these words, and you definitely need to hear such gifts from the folks that you love, too.

Remember that God's glue is everywhere. All at the same time and so accessible and so under used, wasted, and thrown away. Best use up your never-ending supply of God's glue every single day, as going on without your loved one is going to be a new experience.

And now you know that you can always call up your loved one's spirit to come and guide you and love you. Now you can see that the good-byes are not really that at all. They are simply a process of learning to talk to your loved one on a different plane and from a distance, the distance called love.

Don't you see the glory and the honor that you are giving to yourself through this process? Don't you see the homage that you are paying to your loved one? Don't you see the beauty in this time together at this very precious moment?

Don't you see the love that you are giving away and also receiving in return? Don't you know that God wants you to do this so that you can make your life much easier? Don't you and can't you just see the love in all this? I can.

The magic of saying good-bye is learning to be open to the tomorrows. And the tomorrows are always filled with new loves. You will miss these if you haven't said your good-byes and your hellos to your new self and to the others that you will meet.

And always remember that waving good-bye is really waving or motioning for new spirits and entities to come into your life. And angels coming from afar just prevent future glare from sights and happenings yet unseen.

THE MAGIC OF STOP, LOOK, AND LISTEN

(**Author's note:** At the time of a death, I have to look at myself once again and at how strong I am. Many times I have had to be strong although I felt very weak, weary, and worn out. But death and its surrounding circumstances does not care what I think and feel. It's going to happen and someone is going to leave my life. Does it get easier? Never! Am I protected? Definitely!)

This will be the ultimate test of your strength. It will be the reflection on a great portion of your life that was spent with your loved one who is now dying. Are you up to it? I doubt that you can even begin to imagine what this time will be like.

It will be the most powerful thing you have done. And there is no turning back when it comes to death. I'm the only constant in your life, an angel sent from afar. Ain't this grand?

What to do when someone is dying? Simple! S*top, look, and listen.* Do not proceed across any intersections when traffic of any type is approaching. See how simple it is to just live life according to my rules?

Stop your feelings and your doubts. There is no need to fear any of these when you have the immediate answers to describe all of them. You definitely know that I am with you and that I am staying until your moment of death.

Remember? I told you that this time (or at the moment of your death) I will go with you. And we talked about how this was meant to be and how it is slightly unusual for an angel to do this for a human. This is just a gift of what you mean to me.

Look at the beauty of the experience. Look at the wisdom that God is choosing to give to you and your loved one. Look for the glory.

All this beauty. All this pain. All the sorrow imaginable is always present in your earthly trials and tribulations. Why not look at it? Why not touch it? Why not look, learn, and then become?

And you certainly know what you would have missed if you would not have chosen to hear me, look at me, and at times even touch me? Once you looked and knew that I was ever present, the world with me became much clearer to you.

<u>Listen</u> to the voices inside and outside of you, especially those of your spirits. There will not be a bad moment if you do this.

And when you carefully listen, then you will be able to hear us sing. And what's more important, is that you will then learn our songs, our ways, and our meanings. When this is done, then we will all begin to be one. Listening is really singing along with me and always in perfect harmony.

What beauty you have! What hearing you have! All of these will be all you need to thrive and to continue to grow.

Always remember that fear is not a word and has no meaning. It's simply the spirits knocking on your mind and asking to be let in to help.

Simple is as simple is. And that's you and me together. It is simple and do-able. Sure, it's you and me together. And you can do that. All you need is my company, my simple angel being who has come to help you.

You have all the power that you will need—physical, monetary, and psychological. What to do with it is to simply stop, look, and listen. You have learned to be still and to stop what you are doing and now know how to be with us. You look everywhere for answers, and always listen with the utmost care. See, you are the power; and we are the way.

What I am talking about is easy. It is the beauty of the moment and the experience of it. Not to worry. The heavens will open, and all the help you need will come pouring forth; and all of it is God's gift to you.

Within all of this is the love to draw upon. And there's the peace and glory to find. There's never going to be a doubt in your mind. All of this will be the journey of a dream. And it is a dream of love.

Tell it like it is. Play it like it is. Live it as it is. All's well. See, it's simple. This is all you'll need. Just keep all of this knowledge near you.

In the future, I will just become stronger and more communicative and instantly give you feedback without your asking. I will immediately give you all the strength you need. There will never be a doubt for you to waste energy on. I will be your angel dust to protect you in every situation. No fears needed when an angel's about. See, it is simple.

This is going to be magic beyond your wildest dream—the magic of me and you and you and me together. See, I knew you were going to need all this magic and oh, so soon—the power of magic and me and God.

It is the magic of not knowing and letting it take you where and how you need to go. It is the magic of the moment. It is the magic of life and death and love and hope and me.

Go get out that naughty notebook of yours, and let's plan a life for you. Let's make it about love. Let's make it about feelings. Let's make it about you and me together with all the signs and symbols from afar. Let's make it magical. And I am talking about God's magic and not your earthly mumbo-jumbo.

THE MAGIC OF THE CHRISTMAS HOLIDAY

(**Author's note:** Christmas was always one of my most favorite times of the year. But as I got older and the prior generation started to die off, I realized that I didn't have the energy and the desire to continue to keep up all of the traditions that I had helped to create. Thus Christmas became a burden and a holiday to avoid. And, of course, that empty chair at the dinner table was a clear message of more to come. Therefore, holidays have been recreated at my house. Some for the better; some for the worse.)

Holidays are simply days like any other on your planet. The emphasis that is placed upon them is unprecedented in my present world. And to look at holidays from your point of view seems surreal.

The holiday seems to get buried in your media hype and in your structured world of oughts and to-dos and shoulds. Everyone seems to have an opinion of what the other person should be doing to prepare for the event and how much she should spend and where to get the gifts. It seems to be a time of demands being made on a fragile person (called a human being); and after a death, that being certainly ain't up to steam.

Steam has a lot to do with the holidays, too. It seems to me to be a lot of hot air about a really airless event. How can Christmas, for example, be a day that produces so much anxiety and stress and exhaustion?

Christmas is simply a magical time about a blessed event. How can all your media time be filled with all this hype and hot air about a mythical occurrence? On the other hand, then you all turn around and say that you don't totally believe in magic. How can this be?

The magic within any holiday is simply within yourself. It isn't out there somewhere. It isn't in what someone implies that you should do. It isn't within a specific religion or a special ceremony. It isn't mythical and elusive. It's just you.

Getting past yourself may be the real magic of that special day. Your heart knows and remembers yesteryears and their joys and sorrows. The heart is a wonderful vessel of potential joy and hope and magic, too.

If within your heart you can find your magical self—you know that special person that God made—then you might begin to realize that the holiday that you are about to experience is one of wonderment and a very blessed event within itself. That event is the rediscovery of a new person, a person probably buried in memories and yesteryears.

This holiday season I beg you to go within and rediscover yourself. Find that special person who is still floating around somewhere in grief and in sadness and is lacking normal energy and enthusiasm. I want you to look for the little child within yourself.

I want you to take that child out and to love it and to honor it, just as the Christ child is being remembered. I want you to look at what a blessed being you truly are. I want you to love and to give your gifts of love to yourself. I want you to be better to yourself than you have ever been.

I want you to honor and to remember God's most blessed gift, you. Therein lays the magic of your holidays.

THE MAGIC OF THE DOWN TIME

(**Author's note:** A death wears me down—mentally, physically, and spiritually. Consequently, I have many days where I am nearly unable to move. And usually I spend a great deal of time helping other survivors and fail to recognize that my cup is not running over. I learned that writing is my best way of really hearing what Wise Eagle is telling me. Sometimes just giving in to a feeling is my task for that particular day and just going with the emotion is being kind to me.)

Oh, the down time! That special and unexpected time right after an event when you're just sure that you're going to be elated and euphoric and gleeful. Not! Most often your feelings are just the opposite or even worse than you expected.

You may have just buried your loved one or you may have just finished some much-hated book work or legal papers. Or you may have just finished a task around your house and yard. Whew! That job's done. Won't have to do that for a while! Yes! Now on to bigger and better and more pleasurable tasks. Ha!

Then as the sun rises for you on a brand new morning, you just ain't feelin' too great or too enthusiastic about your day. Everything looks good. You've regained some energy, hopefully. You're looking better and a little more rested. But something's out of sync. And that something is you.

You're not a new person today. You're that same old being that's been slightly battered and abused, perhaps both physically and psychologically by the stress that you've lived through. You're not up to par. You're not excited. You're not enthused about another task that absolutely must be done. Sounds like down time to me.

Us angels love humans' down time. We see this as one of the greatest gifts that you can give us. Now you can just give up and either go sleep or play or dream away your day. And now we can be a part of making you all that you can be today.

Now we know that you're not going fritzing [sic] around at top speed and almost so fast that we can't keep up with you. Now we finally have a chance to catch up to you and get you to listen—really, really listen to our messages. Yes, down time is really angel time.

This is the time when you're more than likely to be introspective. This is the time that you'll probably be making lots of "I wonder . . ." statements or "I just wish that . . ." or "If only someone would come help me do . . ." Yes, we hear; and we're listening ever so carefully. You see down time is really angel gift time.

Now, my dear, all you have to do is find a quiet place to sit down and to make that long marvelous list, you know that wish list of all the things that would make your day go better. Then all we have to do is read over your shoulder, assign each wish to one of your special angels, and wham-o we can quickly do our jobs and fulfill all those glorious wishes for you. And, more importantly, make everyone of them come true. Isn't this exciting? It certainly is for us!

Down time is simply the most marvelous gift that you can give us angels. We like making dreams come true. So, my lovely lady, just wish your time away. And then watch, look, and listen for the results to appear.

Have we ever failed you yet? No! Would we do that to you, you who is so very special to us? Never! We're just a dream away, a wish away, a love that's waiting to be delivered. The best is yet to come!

THE MAGIC OF THE LOVE AFFAIR

(**Author's note:** My favorite singer, John Denver, so often sang about love and life and what was true for him. I can see him on the other side, just nodding and saying, "I told you so." So love does make the world go round. All I have to do is look and listen for it.)

The love affair! Yes, this phrase is an attention getter of such proportions. Love, yes, love. Love is my favorite word and one that I hope that I created. Oh my, do I ever like the word, love.

Now just notice what's going on in your mind. There's that ever-so anxious feeling and thought, "Wow, now he's really going to tell all." It's more than that, much more than that.

The love affair that I am referring to is the one that God created for you. It's an explosion. It's an eruption. It's a perfectly glorious morning full of vibrant sunrise colors. And it's also an approaching evening.

It's just watching the glorious colors, the sounds, and the beauty of a peaceful sunset painted on the horizon and all the peace that that signifies for the coming evening. And then the repeating of this same unbelievable process for your bright new day that you call tomorrow.

Wow! Even this word just doesn't describe what I saw and can now see. Don't you just sense in these words how even I'm stumbling over the earthly terms to depict this beauty of God?

Each day, each second of your life you are repeatedly given this love affair to behold and to treasure and to enjoy. Even before your conception, God and you entered into an affair to be shared and to be cherished. This was a gift given so freely and so beautifully.

This was such a special moment that you shared. At this point in time, you both agreed to share your lives. And you both agreed to always be there for each other. At that second, you agreed to always love, honor, and to cherish each other and all that was given to each of you.

In a sense, you entered into a peaceful gift of love and torrid passion. All to be experienced and to be shared with each other and the universe. You agreed to marry and to bury each other with love and compassion. You agreed to be the oneness of your lifetimes together. And you agreed to be free.

But this freedom came with gifts attached. What more could you hope and dream about? Gifts plus freedom? Yes! But then the freedom became something else for you—one of choices, free will, wanderings, and wonderings.

You were given the gift of being your own person. Thus you became an individual. And somewhere along the line you began to forget your first so-called marriage with God and the universe and looked for human beings to be at one with. That was all fine and good, except you began to drift into the world of man and all those earthly obstacles.

Throughout your lifetime on earth you realized that every gift that you possessed and experienced came with different wrapping paper. And some were much prettier and more appealing than others. And some were much larger than life.

Once you unwrapped your treasured gifts, you began to see that there was always pain in addition to the gain. Soon you learned to discern what was good and what was bad. Big mistake.

That judging quality always created another gift of what to do and how to be and then what to do with all this knowledge. In the process, your life became more complicated and confusing.

"Not to worry," I say. "Ha," you say, "this is just plain tough to live with." We were both ever so right.

Love always creates more love and then problems. I call those things gifts given from me to you. And they're called the gifts of life. They're the moments in time that I am most with you. They're the happenings that test your being. They're the most beautiful gifts of all. And one of these is death.

Death, just a simple word that you understand all too well. Death...just an event! Just an experience; just as your life has been. Death, a gift beyond your wildest beliefs. Death, something that I perceive of as the biggest gift of all.

Why on earth would I give you something that I wouldn't perceive of as the utopia of my world? Remember, I have always been in your life. And at this point in time, I am ever closer—ever more loving, ever holding you even closer and tighter.

Why would I give you this gift if I were going to walk away and leave you to suffer at the time of a death? How can you even imagine that I would give you a gift without giving you another one at the same time?

What is this gift? It's more of the gift of you. When your loved one left your world, I immediately saw that now was the time for you to begin to realize the gift that you are to yourself and to me. Now was the time to help you grow ever closer to me.

The problem with this whole death scenario is that man has told you that death is something to be avoided at all cost and that life is the thing to hold on to. Not! Death is not a tragedy. Death is not failure. Death is not a loss of life. Death is not the end. Death is me.

Your loved one is just simply with me. I didn't say that he could never be with you again. I never said that he was unavailable to you. I never told you that you were now alone.

I never told you that you couldn't ever love and be with this person again. I never said that all was over. I never said that this was the end. You and your world told you that. Let's set the record straight once and for all.

Your loved one was your love affair on earth. But remember that you, too, had this first love affair with me! So, now you have had two great affairs. What a blessing! What a couple of gifts! What a miracle!

First, there's the miracle of our relationship and torrid love for each other. Then, on earth, you had a physical affair. Isn't that grand? More than one lover; more than one gift. Miracles and love and gifts are all tied together and cannot be separated.

When I gave you the miracle of life, I also gave you future love affairs and even more earthly gifts. And then you lost sight of this fact. You began to assume (take that word apart and what do you see…ass-u-me) that these things were permanent and would always be present.

Yes, your love affair and that miracle are always and will forever be present. But at no point in time did I tell you that the gift of your loved one was anything more than another miracle and another gift, just like you and me. You believed that that person would always be standing beside you in the physical world. That notion was never meant to be passed on to you.

I gave you heavenly meanings to all these terms and happenings. You gave them earthly meanings that are now not serving you too well. All that is changeable. All that is another miracle and a gift from me to you.

Your loved one lived out the script for his time on earth. Your loved one was put in your life for a reason. Your loved one was just what I wanted for you. That individual was a gift to you. And he is still a gift to you.

Now you can be with him in the spirit world. Now you can communicate in a truly more passionate fashion. Now you can have him with you 24 hours a day. Did you ever experience that on earth? I don't think so.

So what's your problem? You now have the ultimate gift of his presence all the time. You have perfect communication always with love, always with total and instant understanding, and now you always know what the other one's thinking.

Just go and compare that with what you had with this individual on earth. At no time did you have perfect love and communication in your relationship. Now you have the very best gift of all. Now he is a spirit and is always perfectly with you. I told you this would happen. Remember?

Now you have no choice in your survival. Now you must listen to me. Now you must know that life and death are one. They're both experiences, nothing more and nothing less.

Now you must realize that both are simply gifts. Now you must know that both were promised and have been delivered. Now, for you to go on with your remaining time on earth, I am forcing you to believe even stronger in me and my miracles and my gifts. Now you must believe in the spirit world and guardian angels.

Your love affair with me is ongoing. Your affair with your loved one is the same thing. You've always believed in me, and yet you can't seem to remember my physically standing by your side.

Well, your earthly loved one did stand by your side. And now he's just in my world and waiting for your arrival. Call him up. He'll come. He's no different than me. We're both your best and truest lovers.

We're still with you all the time. We're no farther away than we've ever been. We're still the same. We still love you. We still want the best for you. Ask and we will come. Talk to us, just as you've always done.

We're still with you. We're still the lovers that we want to be. Come and be mine...and be mine...and be mine.

THE MAGIC OF THE NUMBNESS OF KNOWING

(**Author's note:** The knowings that I have experienced far surpass any college degree that I have earned. And when this happens, I always feel strung out, up tight, hard wired, and beyond knowledgeable. As a result, my whole body goes into a red alert or a stage of overkill. Then the numbness becomes so overwhelming that I am sure that I am insane. But, all it is, is the intense knowledge of what I am being given and my poor earthly body then goes into overload. An overload of knowings. Not to worry. All is right in the universe.)

More numbing out. More of that old feeling as though some special entity has given you more angel dust than you can handle. It's almost a feeling as though you're frozen inside and unable to call up other feelings and the energy to do the needed tasks for today. What a blessing!

Welcome to the numbness of knowing and all of that special magic of the moment. What a time for you! It's a knowing that soon all of this work and the feelings surrounding your loved one's death may be in the past. It's a knowing that once the paperwork and the legal things are done that the book just may be closed on these types of feelings.

In a sense, it's a relief. On the other hand, it's also a sense that your loved one just may never have been a part of your life. All of these are true and are important.

A feeling word and an intellectual knowing both at the same time always resorts in a sort of confusion. Then you begin to wonder, "Can I do this? Am I capable? What about the mistakes that I could make? What about this weird feeling?"

Well, what about the knowing that you have that you are perfectly o.k.? This is the best part. At no time during the death of your loved one have you been anything less than absolutely o.k.

You know that the love that surrounds you is real. You have the presence of your loved one's spirit. You have your spiritual beings with you. And, of course, you've always had God available, too. Wow! Such a team to join you in this process; a heavenly body of such proportions!

This magical numbness is one that is meant to be. It visits you to tell you, "Hey, you in there, we love you. We're with you. We know you're struggling. We know the feeling. We know the thoughts. We care. Ask us! We will come."

Just the cute little smile on your face as you read this tells me that you're o.k. That smile says to me that you're definitely going to be all right. Sometimes just the knowing that someone is watching and waiting for you is all that you need.

You see this feeling and this knowledge are just gifts from afar. Today they're your gift of magical knowing that the numbness is my presence with you. Know that I am taking your hand and gently asking you to follow me. Follow me where I go...follow me....follow me....follow me.

My footsteps won't be too big for you step into. My feet are the same size as yours. My wisdom now far surpasses yours, but with my intense guidance yours may soon surpass mine.

My arms are wide and warm and welcoming. They will carry you if need be. Otherwise they will link with yours, and we'll walk on together. Sometimes we may even run and gallop. Now that's a thought!

Numbness is magic, as well as the knowing. And all of this is encased in angelic love. Maybe, just maybe, we've sent too much to you, and today's extreme numbing out may be over love. Hmmmm, best I check my love gauge and readjust it to your earthly level of presence. Sometimes we angels overdo what we most love to do—send our love your way.

Please just hold tightly to today's feelings, and I'll gear down my love meter. Dumb thing loves to have its own way. And maybe, just maybe, it is really set at the right level of intensity.

THE MAGIC OF THE SILENCE

(**Author's note:** I remember returning home after my loved one had died. I remember how the silence and the lack of movement in the house were so profound. It was a painful silence, one that said that over half of my life was done; and that book had been closed. I never knew what the word, silence, meant until then. Later I learned that silence was given to me for a reason. Who do you know that's ever written a book with hordes of angel people waiting to be heard?)

The magic of all this silence within you and your home are such precious gifts. They tell you of the time when there were other voices, and there were sounds to be heard, both pleasant and unpleasant.

One generally tends to remember the pleasant voices, those of love and hope and support. Those were the good times. At that point in time, you felt truly loved and felt that you were valued. You could communicate with your loved one in an oh, so, special manner. There were givings and takings. There was love.

There was someone here for you all the time. There were noises in your home. Yes, there were tears even then; but there was that magical thing called hope, too. Hope that things could be worked out and that the future just might hold a time for you to be yourself and to be accepted as such. Now this is all gone for this lifetime.

Now you return home from happy occasions to a very quiet and a very dark house, that is until you turn on the lights. Turning on the lights within your new and different home (one that is now inhabited only by you) is what this magic is all about. In that silence, there is a light; and one that only you can turn on to enjoy. It is bright. It is glorious. It is you and only you.

Yes, the house is silent. Yes, the good times seem as though they're all gone. Yes, you'll feel like this will never change. Yes, it is quiet; but within that quiet is a very powerful message. Yes, even through those tears of yours there are things to hear, things to learn, and things to understand. You see the quiet is only temporary. There is much to know, so much to understand.

The true silence of what you're experiencing is only from your vantage point. You do not see all the activity and all the electrical impulses that exist all around you. All you hear are the sounds that you make.

The occasional phone call that comes in. The infrequent dripping of the water faucet. The occasional sighing of the wind outside. And possibly any noises that your beloved pet may generate. But, wait, that's not all there is. Believe me, I know.

All the magic that surrounds you is from millions of beings from past lives and other generations. If you could only begin to recognize all the fluttering that's going on around you. If you knew about all the voices that are trying to be heard by you. If you could see all those very special beings who want to know you better and to guide you. If only....

My goodness, your house is truly cluttered with beings that are yet unseen and definitely unlistened to. I am just one tiny voice in this wilderness that you're calling a silence. Don't you think that all this cluttering and chattering are worthy of being heard? I definitely do.

The silence within your house is only heard by you. We, the spirits, find it rather crowded living here with you; but, of course, we don't take up much of your air space as we are in a different form.

What you can't see is truly what you can and should get. The wisdom here with so much to learn doesn't begin to tell you what I'm talking about. If you spent one day with this war council of powerful figures, you'd truly wish and hope that they would all shut up and just let one entity talk.

You have no idea what I'm fielding in terms of input. You've given and allowed me the awesome task of speaking for all of them. It's a good thing that my computer brain is now so widely advanced that I am capable of doing this. My friend, the spirit world of silence is never silent.

The magic of the silence is in the sitting and/or standing silently and letting all the elements come together so that this wisdom here can be understood. We've all come to tell you how much you're truly loved. We've all come to guide your way. We've all come to be your bestest friends, and we'd all like to be able to do our jobs.

In the silence of this moment, please listen to our pleas. Please be with us in this silence and let us tell you of times past and other loves. Please let us be a part of you and your life. Please ask for what you need.

Please listen for our answers. Please let us love you and hold you and cradle you in our loving arms. Please let us be in your silence with you so that we can heal your broken heart once again.

We're God's glue sent to mend your heart and mind. We're really good. Please let us be your magic of that silence in your heart, your mind, and your home. Once you let us do this, your silence truly does become magic.

THE MAGIC OF THE SILENCE
OF THE NIGHT

(**Author's note**: I have always equated silence with aloneness. Maybe I should start thinking differently. Maybe silence is really something else. Maybe I was blessed with my loved ones around me. Maybe I should have learned more about such silence as a child. Maybe I am too old to learn about this. Maybe I don't have a choice. Maybe my feelings will change.)

What a magical time, the night! There's a softness in its presence as God puts so many things to sleep and to rest for a period of time. As the sun fades, things become easier to tolerate. In the summertime, the heat diminishes, and the nighttime creatures appear. The birds go to sleep. And out come things like the crickets and the cicadas.

In the wintertime, the air becomes crisper. The winter sounds become more prominent; for example, the crunching of the snow under your feet. The sky becomes much clearer, and the stars shine just a little bit brighter and appear to be close enough to touch.

Sometimes death changes your perspective of all this. As the sun disappears, often times your emotions do not go to sleep. Instead they become more heightened and want to play havoc with your life. They almost seem to run amuck. And the silence changes into something that is dreaded.

During your daytime hours, you seem to be able to tolerate your loved one's absence. You're awake and pursuing some activity. Sure, your heart may not be in that activity at all times; but something compels you to continue to accomplish tasks. Such activity gives a meaning and some sense of purpose to your days.

Then the day turns to night. Maybe you're alone for the first time in your life. Maybe you're not use to entertaining yourself during these quiet hours. Maybe you really and truly don't think that the night will ever end. Maybe the day will never come again. Maybe you are use to illogical thinking. Maybe you're just plain afraid. Maybe you've never been taught to see the magic of the night.

What's there to learn? Oh boy! Loads! Nighttime is the time to bask in the silence of the dark. Now is the time to tell yourself that you're really a big person. It's after dark, and you can do anything that you want to do.

Remember as a kid when you had to come in when it became dark. Just remember how many times that that didn't make any sense to you. Now there is another whole new world to your day, and you're supposed to follow someone else's rules. Not anymore!

The rules of the night are now yours. You're free to go anywhere, do anything. This is where the magic begins. The love of one's self is where you begin to build your own new and different magic of the night.

Find your most deeply desired activity or inactivity. This is where you'll find your new and different love—yourself. Just know that the magic is you. You are the night. You are the silence. You are God's plan for the night. Whatever you conjure up is the magic of the silence of the night.

THE MAGIC OF THE SPINNING

(**Author's note:** Many days I wasn't home mentally. I wasn't anywhere else either. I was just spinning around and choking on tears and fears. I had to be the biggest spinning top in the Midwest. On those days all I could do was write about it. And once I saw the feelings on paper, I knew that I was still o.k. and alive. I wasn't going anywhere very fast, but I was moving; and Wise Eagle was holding my hand.)

This is a whole lot like your mind running wild when you are all alone even when you're not alone. Where does the mind go and when does it return? That's the magic of its spinning.

The spinning of the mind is like the angels coming and stirring up your brain with a magical spoon. Wheeeee! Can't you just get a picture of that happening? Maybe I should write a children's book depicting this magical occurrence, colored pictures and all.

Here are these mystical beings saying, "Hello, I'm here to confuse you in the most delightful way. Boy, I sure hope that this individual will also notice my efforts, ask for my help, and end up feeling euphoric and gleeful after this experience is analyzed."

What happens? Simple! The dust of the angels is sprinkled throughout your mind—all the thoughts, the feelings, the hopes, the events, etc. On first glance, you think that this is a huge mess. Not!

It's just the magical spinning of all the glorious events and feelings surrounding death. It's like a basket of kittens that are squirming every which way and crying and twisting and crawling all over each other to get some other place.

What does this prove for you? It proves that you're alive and well and functioning. Angel dust will do it to you every time. It's meant to be this way.

What should you do with this magical spinning? First, and most important, is to know that it's just your beloved spirit guides coming to tease you a bit so that you will notice them and hear them and sense them about and most importantly ask them for help and then listen and do what they tell you.

They are never wrong. They are always close by. They want to help you all the time. They've come to say that they love you. They want you to come play with them. They want you to be well and able to function. They want you to ask for help and be accepting of it.

The mind never runs wild. You are never alone. You are always loved and cared for. You are always a child of God. You are everything that I want you to be. You are the magic in the spinning. You are me!

THE MAGIC OF THE WAITING

(**Author's note:** "Your loved one is going to die this evening," the nurse said. So what should I do? What are the rules that I should follow? There are none, so don't ask. And so I sat and patiently waited and wondered how many other people in the world were doing a similar thing that evening. The following essay is what I heard. It didn't seem like a magical time to me. But since Wise Eagle told me that it was, I had to believe him. Maybe I missed some of the magic.)

Waiting is a gift, one of divine intervention. It is a time for the mind to slow down and to process the cherished moments with your loved one. It's a time of joy. It's a time of sadness. It's a time of being at peace and at one with God.

Waiting is a little like hope. It's not an anticipated time. It's one of such upheaval that one could misconstrue its meaning.

Waiting is hope—hoping for more time; hoping for less time; and hoping for the best for everyone. It's a little like that paralyzing feeling, almost undefinable [sic] but yet one of such great value.

Waiting is the being at one with your feelings and your thoughts. That's a time of looking inward and collecting all your best memories and then looking at each of them very lovingly and gently and then placing them back in their appropriate place in your heart.

Waiting isn't all that it's cracked up to be. Sometimes it can be unbearable and way too long. During those times you will truly wonder if you are losing your mind. Not to worry!! If you lose it, God will do more than his best to make sure that you find it. In addition, he will so lovingly help you to get it all back in order and to treat yourself to a new and better you.

Waiting is the gift that God creates for you to learn to love yourself. It's a time for you to realize the magnitude of the gift that you are!

THE MAGIC OF THE WAVES

(**Author's note:** What rules should you follow to grieve? You can read all the books on grief and loss, just as I had done, but the answer is more like "Duh?" Nothing seemed to fit for me, so I fumbled through. Some days I was immobile and simply typed funny lists. Every day seemed to have a new list to record. And my friends soon began to believe that I had gone over the edge. But where is that edge? Maybe I went over it and just stayed there. I definitely lost my way to where? And I don't know where I was going.)

Death is all about waves, and their coming and their going, with or without you. Last night there were waves of tears when you went to bed. In fact, they put you to sleep and also awakened you this morning. You didn't see them as anything good or comfortable. I saw them as God's way of cleaning up the messes in your life.

And cleanliness is right next to Godliness, just as your mother preached to you. Now, if you'd only listened much more closely to the symbolism of everything that she tried telling you... and so it goes. But your part-time listening to her now just gives me a chance to teach you in the most delightful way, my way.

Your waves of emotional waves are all perfectly normal, natural, and so enlightening. Let's see, there are:

Waves of waves
Waves of heavy waves
Waves of wakefulness
Waves of panic
Waves of not knowing
Waves of loneliness
Waves of not loving him
Waves of feeling sorry for him
Waves of suddenness

Waves of emotions
Waves of crumbling
Waves of crying
Waves of overload
Waves of fears
Waves of nothingness
Waves of livingness [sic]
Waves of silence
Waves of hard waves
Waves of huge waves
Walls and walls of waves

For you, the waves of not knowing were the worse. Most of the time, you were blessed with not realizing the repercussions of the impending death. Thank God that some days you were only able to zero in on making lists of things. Lists of lists, and lists of haunting memories and what ifs.

These vast and extensive lists (that I was totally left out of) sometimes frightened your loving friends. They didn't know what they meant. Neither did you. I knew exactly that they were all lists that dealt with the not knowings of your life—those of yesterday, those of today, and those of yet-to-come.

Again I must say that death will always do this to you. It is like a catalyst that draws everything into a more sincere and acute focus. It is even more than this. It is having a 20-20 vision capacity, but in the dimension where I live. This is definitely being blown away home, with or without your permission.

And most deaths do occur without your permission. And thus the waves begin immediately. Waves of waves of memories, feelings, and experiences. And throughout this process, you realize that you have no control of anything or anyone. And just ain't that a blessing?

Then you will know and realize that you are the ebb and the tide and that you will soar above the swells. Float away the day.

You're a wall of strength; a fortress that will receive the waves and then throw them back to God. So just who has the power and the control?

Waves of anything can never hurt you. All you have to do is ask to be held up against the rip tide. I can do this for you and so can God. Ask for protection and assistance with the waves, the ebb, the flow, and the blessed relief that they offer.

Where do I hide and where can you instantly find me? In the waves, in their breaking, and in their undertow. I am with you in every blast of waves that engulf you and leave you standing, cleaned, and redressed. I am in all that you see and know and feel. I am the inner glow in all of this.

Therefore, look at your waves. Tell them to come closer. Ask them to clean you, once and for all. Let them see you as you are. And then look in front of yourself, to both sides, and behind you. What do you see? Angels everywhere and hardly a place for more to stand.

We are the waves. We are in your not knowings. We are the wind that stands you tall. We are the sun that dries the moisture. We are the moon that lulls you into peaceful waves of more to come.

We are the love within your waves of not knowing. We are the love that sees you home each day and refreshes you each night. We are the magic in your waves. Won't you come join us?

THE MAGIC OF THIS IS ALL THERE IS

(**Author's note:** How much more could I deal with? Thank God I only had one death to deal with this time. Knowing that deaths frequently come in threes, I immediately asked, "Is this all there is?" And the answer was, "Yes." And then I realized that this second is all that I truly need to survive. What I have right now is more than enough for me. And, thank God, I had fleets of angels to see me through, as I could never have done it alone.)

The phrase, this is all there is, is pretty powerful. It indicates the presence of a supreme being who is making doubly sure that this second, this point in time, is a gift to you and a blessing bestowed.

Just imagine! That blessing is given to you billions and trillions of times over your lifetime. It's never ever withheld. It's never anything less that perfect. It's never something that you have to look for. It's always there, always a gift, and always free. And it is always magical.

The giver of this magic is someone that loves and protects you from all harm. Oh, yes, it certainly seems different at times. Occasionally, it appears as though this person is out to get you. Wrong!

Never, ever would he do that to you. He always remembers the gift that you are to him. Likewise, he remembers so well the gift that he created for the world.

And this world needs every gift of you. You in all your times of misery. You in all your times of glory and success. This world can only be as good as you are. You are that special entity that makes the world magical.

God knows that you are struggling. God knows that you are questioning the present. God knows that nothing can change that feeling unless you find the magic of this moment.

God shows you this each moment. He tells you this by keeping you alive. He shows you the way, through his love and caring. He tells you to be ever near to him and to let your guardian angels become more visible and helpful.

Simple, you say? Difficult your mind tells you. Simple—I tell you! Remember that simple is as simple is. Now is as now is.

Every moment has special thoughts and feelings. Each of these is for a definite reason and is not to ever be discounted, denied, or ignored.

What should you do? Why, there's only one thing to do. Find a favorite place to sit down and be very quiet and reflective. Begin to listen. Really listen and ask all the questions that you have.

Now, just whom are you going to ask? You're going to ask your favorite loved ones, both dead and alive, to come and be with you and to guide you. Hocus Pocus, you say? Not!

If you want help from friends and family in your earthly world, you ring them up, don't you? Well, now you're going to do the same thing with the spirits. If you never directly ask, you never directly receive.

I'm telling you that you must do this! These favorite individuals surround you all the time. They're there just waiting for a message from you and want to help you in any way possible. This makes their lives a gift to you.

And by your asking them to help you, you give them the gift of you. Isn't that what your world is all about? Sharing the gifts that you are with each other and basking in the knowledge that you will never be denied.

You ask then what is the magic of this is all there is? It's everything. It's everybody in the spirit world that surrounds you all the time. It's the gift you are to yourself and to your loved ones. It's the knowledge that this is all that is needed for this moment to be magical. It's all about asking and receiving and watching and looking for the signs to guide your way.

It's about you and me together. It's about love and hope and peace. It's all about the magic and the knowledge that <u>this is all there is</u>. This has been and always will be quite enough for you to continue to grow and love and live and to be the gift that you are to yourself and your world.

THE MAGIC OF TOMORROW

(**Author's note:** As my loved one was dying, I knew that I was going to be the one standing alone by his grave site. Something that I definitely told God that I didn't want to do! Damn, he wasn't listening to me again. Therefore, my mission was to buck up and get through the days. My motto was the same as always. Try harder and you can make things better. Not so. And so I wrote. And when I did, all was made clear to me. And the magic of the message was there's magic in everything, but some days Wise Eagle had to make this true for me.)

Tomorrow seemed so far away. And this was true every day of the dying process. And if it was coming, you certainly could care less about it. And, no, those days weren't all a blur, but they were certainly filled with chaos and weird feelings.

Getting up was the same each day. Putting on your clothes and washing your face were the same. Feeding the kitty was the same. His demands never varied. And you complied and loved him.

Did you eat? You must have, as you're still alive today. Did it matter? Not very many times, as we took over for you and made you appear to be somewhat normal.

What was this process all about? It was the making of the you that you are today. We just took the old you and turned you into something that you had never seen. Let's see, there was the angry you, the sad you, the confused you, the knowing you, and the terribly fearful you.

Need I go on? The you's in your life changed by the second. Actually they changed by the multitude each and every second. There wasn't a you that stayed long enough for you to recognize. Therefore, I'd say that you traveled extensively within your body over those last few days of the dying process. And no one was home in there.

Was there a new tomorrow? Sure, it was yesterday turned inside out and made into a new day. It's like an old sock. If it doesn't feel right when you put it on, then turn it inside out; and it may fit better. Seemed so at the time.

Some tomorrows don't fit. Some are made that way. They're meant to grab you and hold you longer than the last one. They're meant to bind us together. They're meant to require more love from God.

Tomorrow doesn't have to be something for you to know about. It's just a word, a new meaning, nothing too special. But the importance of tomorrow is that you will be different, never ever the same. And if you look for the same you, you will miss this second, this moment.

Therefore tomorrow's magic is the sense that all will be new and true and blue. It is not about better or worse or less than. It's simply about the magical sense of something new. And during the time of a death, new is good and clean and special. Make tomorrow magically much more special than today. Can I help?

THE MAGIC OF WANDERINGS AND WONDERINGS

(**Author's note:** Too many things to do. Too many things to think about. Too many thoughts, feelings, and happenstances going through my mind. Too many unknowns; way, way too many. Too much stress and not enough energy. Thus the lists began again. A wandering mind has a lot of things to wonder about.)

If you don't know where you're going, you're definitely going somewhere via something. For days and days I watched you traverse that mountain, back and forth and forth and back. Yes, you moved. Did you see new scenery? Sometimes, but other times you saw nothing and only felt. You wandered a lot.

When this happens, you just as well make some lists of what you are wondering about. Best just wander around in your mind for that day. And as you go, please remember that I, too, see and know different things about you. And this time you are not going to leave me out of your list making, as I am insisting that you record mine, too. Darlin', stardom does have its price you know and also needs to be fed.

This was your list for one morning. A list of everything that you were wondering about. It contained no answers, nor did you ask for any; but you could have asked me for help.

JAN'S I WONDER...

I wonder if I'm as good as I think I am.
I wonder if I should be feeling all those designated stages
    of grief.
I wonder if they're manifesting themselves in other ways.
I wonder if they're lurking somewhere and going to come
    out and bite me later.
I wonder if there's a voice that I'm not listening to.
I wonder if I should look for that voice.

166

I wonder if I'm insane for even thinking this.
I wonder why I'm feeling so overwhelmed.
I wonder if this is another of Wise Eagle's and God's gifts.
I wonder if I can stand anymore of their gifts.
I wonder if I'm depressed.
I wonder if I'd recognize it.
I wonder if it's worth thinking about.
I wonder if I'm really up and on my feet.
I wonder if I have feet anymore.
I wonder if there's any stable ground to really stand on.
I wonder if I'm mentally ill.
I wonder if there's such a thing as mental health vs. mental
    illness.
I wonder if this is really an issue with me.
I wonder where all this writing is taking me.
I wonder if I want to go there.
I wonder if I should wonder.

While you were writing your list on wonderings, I wrote
my own. As you can see, my wonderings are all about what I can
do for you from a distance. I do global wonderings while you do
up close and personal issues. I see big while you think small.

WISE EAGLE'S LIST OF I WONDER . . . .

I wonder if you truly know that I am here.
I wonder if you'd recognize me if I'd reappear for you.
I wonder if you see the sunshine.
I wonder if you know what the rain really is.
I wonder where your mind is.
I wonder if you have a mind.
I wonder if you'd know the difference.
I wonder if even God could get through to you right now.
I wonder what happened to the dreamer in you.

I wonder what happened to the child that wants to play.
I wonder if the child would recognize you right now.
I wonder if the tears would help you.
I wonder why there's any doubt in your mind.
I wonder why you like these frickin' lists that leave me out.
I wonder if you really care.
I wonder if you love me.
I wonder if you love yourself.
I wonder if love is the issue.
I wonder if the issue isn't changes.
I wonder where you'd like to go with these changes.
I wonder if anything would reach you right now.
I wonder why you're dancing away.
I wonder if the dance is your sadness.
I wonder if sadness isn't a new song.
I wonder if sadness is the right term.
I wonder if the term isn't joys.
I wonder if joys wouldn't ease your weary mind.
I wonder if weariness isn't the issue.
I wonder if the peace that you have recently isn't the issue.
I wonder if peace isn't what is overwhelming you.
I wonder if God couldn't help you.
I wonder if all of us haven't been too much for you.
I wonder if we should stop writing the books for a while.
I wonder if you're concerned if your feet are on this earth
    or if they're really in heaven.
I wonder if the teachings that we've given to you were
    given too rapidly.
I wonder if God would know the answer.
I wonder if you realize your beauty.
I wonder if you've lost sight of the knowledge you now
    have
I wonder if the pain hasn't been worth the gain.

I wonder if there isn't a simple answer.

I wonder if the answer isn't in the process.

I wonder if the process isn't what's to blame for your feelings.

I wonder if you need to decide to banish your earthly copings and come over to just celestial ramblings on how to live and to believe.

I wonder if you're overwhelmed with me.

I wonder if I'm your problem.

I wonder if you'd tell me how to do it differently.

I wonder if you know how special you are to me.

I wonder if I can convey that another way.

I wonder if you realize that each writing is part of a master plan and will be used somewhere in your books.

I wonder if God isn't your answer.

I wonder how you're going to receive the answer.

Lists and questions are good ways to get me to pay attention to your most immediate concerns and worries. I sense your traumatic feelings before I hear your words. I know that this is hard for you to believe, but it is true.

The vibration from your feelings immediately wakes me up—in case I happen to be dozing by your side. Actually sensing this is like being inside of you and realizing just how close you are to going over the edge. I truly know your feelings before they hit your consciousness.

And my job is to immediately hold you closely while you keep wandering farther and farther from a sense of being. How can I do this? Where does all this lead?

Well, first of all, if I don't catch you before you fly away, then your second fleet of angels intercept you and hold you close by until I can find a way to get you to write for me. Of course, this is in case you won't verbally talk to me right then.

Once we can find out just how much you are hurting, we then call out to the universe and to all your other fleets of angels for their input. And, of course, this is immediate feedback for us; and then my part comes into play.

Since I am your number one angel guide and since I am the only one who can speak for all the other concerned and loving angels in your fleet, my second tactic is to try and capture you and talk to you in my beautiful way. Thank God that you have finally given up on questioning everything that you hear from me. What a pain that was!

If I can't get through to you during your waking hours, then I can resort to using the time when you are asleep to intervene. It is much easier if you would write down one of your wonderings on a piece of paper, stick it under your pillow, and ask me for an answer via your dreams or upon your awakening.

But if none of these work, I will definitely pursue. You know, signs and symbols and other electrical impulses to get you to be aware of me and my need to help you. One of my strongest suits is that I never give up, give in, or get down.

The magic of your wanderings and wonderings is that your lists always lead you right back to me. You see, my advice and wisdom are supreme and will always produce the magic that you have gotten so use to. So give me your time, your lists, and your feelings. I can fix them in a second.

I can help you heal your broken heart. The magic is in your meanderings, and I am the best answer you have. And all of these will make you free and help you see the value of being you.

THE MAGIC OF YOUR OWN DEATH

(**Author's note:** My mother said that God sat in heaven with a large book in which was recorded the day that I would die. Of course, she had her own picture in her mind of her time in heaven. But for me as a little girl, this was very frightening. So I learned to fear most everything. And then I discovered higher education and realized that I wasn't alone in my fears and that if I taught about death that I might find the beauty in it. And I did. And I also found that death was nothing to fear.)

Your own death is yours. You can enjoy it. You can abhor it. You can embrace it. You can look forward to it. You can dance and sing. You can rejoice. This choice is truly yours and yours alone. And what a choice it is, too.

Wanting and longing for death are good signs. Then we truly know that you also have that same longing for your life, that anticipation of wonderment, that joy and gleam in your eyes, that overwhelming feeling of peace in your heart and deep within your soul. You see, death and life are pals and not enemies. Knowing that life and death symbolize so very much will bring you peace.

If you could just remember what heaven and God and your angel friends were like, this would make you so joyful and so excited. You see death is this same excitement and even more so than your birth was.

Your birth was traumatic considering your prior heavenly home. You were alone at that moment and no longer with us and sharing our comfort and our arms. No wonder babies cry at their own births. *Never do you hear that a person cries at the moment of death.*

What a life you had before you came to earth. What a memory you aren't allowed to remember; and if so, only in bits and pieces. A pity! And all for very good reasons.

Had you been allowed to remember your prior lives, your present existence would have been colored and would have been less productive in learning terms. That prior life is now one that you long for every day.

For you personally, you've always longed for and wondered about something. Now you fully realize that that something else was your prior lives. And what a joy that has been for me to see the wonderment in your eyes, as a few memories flood back into your awareness.

It's been a beautiful process for me, as I've seen your wide-eyed joy and never pain or sorrows. You've always truly been amazed and so relieved as these memories have answered so many questions about your present life. I have been truly blessed to have been given this opportunity to be the deliverer of blessed memories to you. Thank you for being my angel pal on earth.

We've now decided that when you're ready to come be with us, you can. You can set the time, the moment, the peaceful event. You've earned that right. You've struggled one time enough.

And now for that moment, that blessed, glorious event is what you make it. The choices are all yours now. Isn't that exciting? I'm awaiting, and that should be all you'll ever need to sustain you through all the remaining hard times, all the sadness left in your life, all the changes that are to come about.

The magic of your own death will be all that you want it to be. It is nothing to fear. It is nothing to question. It is nothing to ponder. Just choose the most glorious memories, events, and anticipations and that's what it will be. Simple? Simple is what God is.

Now go on with your glorious life. Live it. Be it. And please include me in it, as well as your other beloved angels from heaven and from earth, too.

Let's take our hands and skip through the days. Let's love each other. Let's be all that you can be. We'll share all of this and always be with you to sing, to dance, and to cry. But with this knowledge, you are now truly free to be with us at all times. Let's go make the world a better place.

THE MAGICAL STAGE OF . . . .

(Author's note: Wise Eagle told me that he would determine when this book was finished and that would be that. The end! And so he did. If I had known from the beginning that I could call up my fleets and fleets of angels to guide me through this life, I know that my life would not have seemed like a continual hell on earth. If I had been praised for my intellect, my creativity, and my psychic abilities, I would never have needed four college degrees to keep going and growing. Was it waste? Of course not. It was all magical, even the pain and the sadness.)

Gotcha! I just bet that you were expecting another one of my monumental and prophetic stages of magic. Wrong! Now all I have left to say to you is that the magic is yours, and all yours to find and to have and to hold.

Where do I begin when I now know that you are so knowledgeable about yourself, your guardian angels, and your Supreme Being? Where is the place for me to carry you through to your next life event? Where do you want to be when it is your time to die? Where is just where all that will occur and what will happen.

By now I'm sure that you have realized that there were no stages of grief, of sorrow, and of your loved one's dying process. There were no stages unless you devised them and lived through them and learned and grew from them. There were no stages. And just when you thought that you understood something about all the processes of death, you had to come up with something that you could live with and live through.

In actuality, there was no format to follow, no steps to see, and no stages to guide you. Nothing! That's life, isn't it? So why wouldn't you expect that from death, too?

Why? Because you believe that in all this process there should be something that others have endured and that applies to you, too. Wrong! Everything is according to plan, and everything is totally unique and you.

See, you are the stages. You make them up. You live through them. Okay, so you muddle and grapple and curse your way through them. Let's get real. They really are a bitch, in most every sense. They're painful. They're unending. They're ever present. They're just plain time consuming and so hard to get a grasp on. They just really are a bitch!

And so the magic is all that you have to turn to to see you through. The magic is the message. It is the recipe. It is the concoction that will feed you and love and hold you through all these times. The magic is you!

And the magic is the ending. It is also the beginning. Now my question to you is what is in between, and how big and how great is that part of what you've just been through?

We all know that it is definitely bigger than a bread basket, deeper than an ocean, and let's don't even go into the part about the mountains that you've climbed. And, far be it from me to tell the world about the mountains that you built for yourself and the effort that you put forth to do it. No need to let everyone know that you created a lot of your hilly spots in your magical mine field.

And in all this mess is also the nowhere stage. Nowhere is better than being somewhere where you don't want to be. This is that place where you are safely and tenderly guarded, guided, and over loved by us angels and by God. It's the place that you have learned to long for and hunted endlessly to find.

In addition, there is the meant-to-be stage, too. This is the place, when at the end of each day, you ask yourself where's the rhyme and where on earth is the reason for all that has transpired.

And when you became all knowing, you were able to say that the death, the feelings, and the happenings were meant to be according to your life script and that of your loved one. It's like saying, "Oh, God, now I get the picture. Why couldn't you have painted it more clearly for me? Yeah, yeah, yeah, all was meant to be this way."

The magic is the way that you deal with you and your loved ones and your world. The magic is you. So now you have learned to find your own magic, to see the lights in the sky that show you the magical way, and to live with yourself. And you are the magical stage called you.

So, when your next loss occurs, you'll immediately go for the magic bottle. You'll see the signs. You'll see the wind. The sun will be the guiding beam for you to illuminate more magic in the vessel called you.

Remember, too, that I have a magical wand and will loan it to you. Do promise to use it frequently and oh, so, well. And always remember I'll be guiding you, and then the angel within you will become even more visible. I told you that you were the magic. Now, just let it shine through!

All you've seen is the magic
All you've longed for is true
All the glory you've wondered about
All of this is just you.